SHAKESPEARE:

TEXT, STAGE AND

CANON

~

THE ARDEN SHAKESPEARE

*Second series

SHAKESPEARE:

TEXT, STAGE AND

CANON

Richard Proudfoot

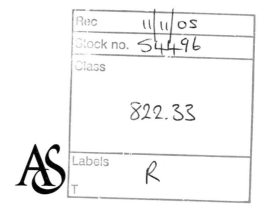

The Arden website is at
http://www.ardenshakespeare.com

Shakespeare: Text, Stage and Canon
first published 2001 by the Arden Shakespeare

© 2001 Richard Proudfoot

Arden Shakespeare is an imprint of Thomson Learning

Thomson Learning
Berkshire House
168–73 High Holborn
London WC1V 7AA

Typeset by LaserScript, Mitcham, Surrey

Printed by Zrinski in Croatia

British Library Cataloguing in Publication Data
A catalogue record for this book is available from the British Library

Library of Congress Cataloguing in Publication Data
A catalogue record has been applied for

ISBN 1–903436–11–7

NPN 9 8 7 6 5 4 3 2 1

For Nicola,
sine qua non

CONTENTS

ACKNOWLEDGEMENTS

The author and publishers are grateful to the following individuals, companies and institutions for permission to reproduce copyright material. Every effort has been made to contact copyright holders and the publishers will be happy to include further acknowledgments.

Illustrations: W.W. Norton and Company, New York and London (p. 10); Thomson Learning (p. 27); Shakespeare's Globe (p. 37); The British Library, 11795 t 85 f7v, Notes (p. 51); Conway Library/Courtauld Institute of Art/The Provost and Fellows of Worcester College (p. 59); Klaus Lefebvre/Bühnen der Stadt Köln (p. 94).

Text extracts: Folger Shakespeare Library (p. 6); Cambridge University Press (pp. 33–4, 42); Routledge (pp. 42–3); Oxford University Press (p. 43); Associated University Presses (pp. 55–6).

LIST OF ILLUSTRATIONS

FOREWORD

by R.A. Foakes

The editor remains unnoticed by most readers of a work, however glad they may be of the help given by the introduction, the commentary notes and useful information organized by someone whose name is printed after the author – William Shakespeare, *Hamlet*, edited by ... well, who cares? Students and readers of literature may not even realize that every work they enjoy has been edited for them, more or less well, by some hard-working scholar whose researches have established the best text and whose knowledge has provided the many aids to enjoyment that they take for granted. If the idea of the editor ever crosses the mind of many students, I suspect it may often be in the scornful fashion of W.B. Yeats in his poem 'The Scholars':

> Bald heads forgetful of their sins,
> Old, learned, respectable bald heads
> Edit and annotate the lines
> That young men, tossing on their beds,
> Rhymed out in love's despair
> To flatter beauty's ignorant ear.
> All shuffle there; all cough in ink;
> All wear the carpet with their shoes;
> All think what other people think.

Editors, of course, are not like this at all. The team of editors gathered by Richard Proudfoot to work on the third series of Arden editions of Shakespeare's plays and poems includes many who are young and hairy and none who have been known to cough in ink, and they possess a variety of opinions that at once demolishes the idea that they think what other people think. The editors that Yeats imagined were all male, but Richard has enlisted women among the Arden editors, one of whom, Ann Thompson, shares with him the work of general editor. The business of editing the plays of Shakespeare and his contemporaries has been a site of extraordinary change and discovery during the twentieth century, and Richard has been involved in these developments throughout his career. He worked for some time on, and energized others also to give attention to, the so-called Shakespeare Apocrypha, a dozen or so plays that were attributed to Shakespeare before the end of the seventeenth century. He also served as general editor of the Malone Society Reprints series of type facsimiles of important Elizabethan and Jacobean plays and documents. It is entirely fitting that his career should culminate in his oversight of the leading scholarly edition of Shakespeare, the Arden third series, now well on its way to completion.

It is also fitting that at his retirement from King's College London he should be invited to distil the wisdom he has gained over the years in the lectures published in the present book. If he is learned, and perhaps respectable now, he has always defied Yeats's image of a scholar, not least by his passion for performance and the stage. He has a long practical experience of acting and directing Shakespeare's plays, and his thinking about Shakespeare is affected both by this experience and by constant theatre-going. His enthusiasm emerges in the second of his lectures, 'staged' appropriately at the recon-structed Globe on Bankside. He is known for the careful and detailed advice he provides to the editors of the plays in the Arden series, advice in which he brings to bear not only his editorial wisdom but also his sense of the plays as texts for performance. Editors who have been aided by his supply of information, his suggestions and queries, always informed by good sense and sound critical principles, acknowledge his help as invaluable.

I have an image of him chairing a meeting of thirty or forty Arden editors; he glances round with a quizzical smile, as if ready to enjoy anything odd or eccentric, and sets discussion going with self-deprecating humour. He has a way of signalling with slightly raised eyebrows and a sceptical look his perception of mistaken views, ignorance or folly in others, as he moves the meeting genially along. At the end all leave feeling they have had a useful and enjoyable time. The same combination of a graceful turn of phrase, level-headed judgement, good humour and good sense, characterize his lectures, which also are nicely orchestrated. No one is better qualified than Richard to take stock of recent advances and future prospects in our understanding of Shakespeare's texts and of Shakespeare's theatres. In this short book he deftly engages with a wide range of current issues, placing them in relation to past developments and discoveries, as well as setting them in the context of current theoretical debates relating to texts, the stage and the Shakespearean canon. The book provides both a needed overview of the latest thinking about these matters at the beginning of a new century, and a point of departure for further advances. Richard writes, as he observes, with the 'practical editor's envy of the theorist's freedom of speculation', and it is a great strength of his book that his discussion is grounded always in history and in the latest understanding of the evidence. At a time when textual theory is preoccupied with indeterminacy, instability and the heady but impractical concept of 'unediting', as if editors somehow constrict texts and terrorize readers, it is especially valuable to have the clear-headed perspective of an immensely knowledgeable practical editor.

PREFACE

These three lectures were delivered, in essentially the form in which they are printed in this book, in October 1999, at the invitation of Jessica Hodge of Thomas Nelson and Sons Ltd, then publishers of the third series of the Arden Shakespeare, and of Patrick Spottiswoode, Director of Globe Education. Their suggestion was that the lectures be given in three different rooms, reflecting their triple occasion. The first, to mark the centenary of publication of the Arden Shakespeare, was given at Stationers' Hall on 6 October. The second, to commemorate the 400th anniversary of the opening of the first Globe theatre on the Bankside, was given on 13 October. It was to have inaugurated the new Nancy W. Knowles lecture theatre at the new Globe, but had to be transferred at short notice to the Bear Garden theatre, as the builders missed the deadline for completion of the new room. The last lecture, on 20 October, in the Great Hall of King's College London, was on the occasion of my retirement from the English Department after thirty-three years.

My deepest gratitude is due both to the two sponsors of the lectures and to the friends and colleagues who kindly chaired them, David Scott Kastan and Ann Thompson at Stationers' Hall; Thomas L. Berger and Andrew Gurr (standing in impromptu for Stanley Wells) at the Globe; and Gordon McMullan and Professor Arthur Lucas, Principal of King's College, at King's. I likewise acknowledge the indispensable contribution to the production of this book made by the unfailingly supportive Jessica Hodge and her colleagues at Thomson Learning and by the brisk and efficient copy-editing of Lynden Stafford.

I chose to reflect on three of my own main preoccupations in the study of Shakespeare: the editing of his plays in the twentieth century; the attempts to recover an authentic stage for the performance of the plays; and the authorship both of the plays habitually attributed to Shakespeare and of some others on the fringe of his canon. These topics seemed apt to the three locations and occasions of the lectures.

The lectures and the published work referred to in their footnotes reflect only a tiny part of my debt to the many students, scholars, actors and others who have contributed so much to my own pleasure and profit during my career as a teacher of English literature, and especially Shakespeare. At a time when all established reputations are open to challenge, it is increasingly alleged that Shakespeare has lost his relevance to life in the modern world. The amount and quality of interest in his plays in the twentieth century, as reflected in my references, leads me to suppose that he has not yet lost his power over audiences and readers – and even, sometimes, over scholars and critics.

Richard Proudfoot
King's College London
June 2000

1

TEXT

The Arden Shakespeare, published by Methuen & Co., began in 1899 with *Hamlet*, priced at 3*s*. 6*d*. Its editor was Edward Dowden, Professor of English at Trinity College, Dublin, and author of the popular *Shakespere: A Critical Study of his Mind and Art* (1875). In the following year he added *Romeo and Juliet*. A team of editors was built up under the General Editorship of Dowden's friend W.J. Craig, some of whom were to edit three or four plays, one, H.C. Hart, as many as seven (including the three parts of *Henry VI*). By 1907 twenty-five volumes were in print: a further nine had been added by 1914. Of the remaining five required to make up a set of thirty-seven plays and two volumes of non-dramatic poetry, two, *Henry VIII* and the *Sonnets*, appeared during the war years, both edited by the Rev. C. Knox Pooler, and the remaining three between 1922 and 1924. Craig died before completing his edition of *Coriolanus*, which was finished by his successor as General Editor, R.H. Case. *Much Ado about Nothing* (1924), the last play in the series, was also the only one to be edited by a woman, Grace R. Trenery.

The Edwardians are now routinely accused of bardolatry, and phrases such as 'Once more we see the shaping sensitive fingers at work' (on the character of Don John in *Much Ado*[1]) are indeed to be found, but these editions are in general remarkable for their coolness and for their focus on the matter in hand. It may be that the series was an understated English response to the academic overkill and heavyweight bulk of the

American New Variorum edition edited by H.H. Furness, in which a single difficult line of text could generate pages of commentary. The short introductions, mostly running to between thirty and fifty pages, waste no space and remain informative on their chosen topics – though those topics, notably the novelistic 'time-schemes for the action' kindly supplied by P.A. Daniel, have not all stood the test of time. The critical focus on character may now appear narrow and at times moralizing or sentimental – but the beginning of the twentieth century was the great age of Shakespeare the novelist.

Dowden's 'Introductory Note' to *Hamlet* was abbreviated into a blurb for the series.

> The aim of this edition of Shakespeare is to meet in some degree the requirements of three classes of readers. There are those who care only to enjoy the play without the retardation or the disturbance of notes; for them a text, which it is hoped may be regarded as trustworthy, is printed in a type which imposes little fatigue on the eye.... There are, secondly, readers who recognise the fact that many difficulties exist in what Shakespeare has written, ... for these readers a body of explanatory notes, in which a mean is attempted between parsimony and superfluity, has been provided. Thirdly, there are scholarly readers, who have a legitimate desire themselves to check or control the work of the editor in the formation of his text.... In 'Hamlet' an attempt is made to exhibit the variations from the editor's text, which are found in the primary sources, the Quarto of 1604 and the Folio of 1623, in so far as those variations are of importance for the ascertainment of the text. Every variation is not recorded, but the editor has chosen to err on the side of excess rather than that of defect.[2]

The comments of reviewers reprinted as testimonials are not trenchant, but those reviewers wrote not only for the *Athenaeum* ('Leaves little to be desired as a model of arrangement and printing; it is light and handy, and eminently readable') or the *Westminster Gazette* ('the binding is chaste but substantial'), but also for the *Daily Chronicle* ('A critical edition of Shakespeare in a thoroughly readable form.... a model of ripe and sane scholarship' – and 'ripeness', we know,

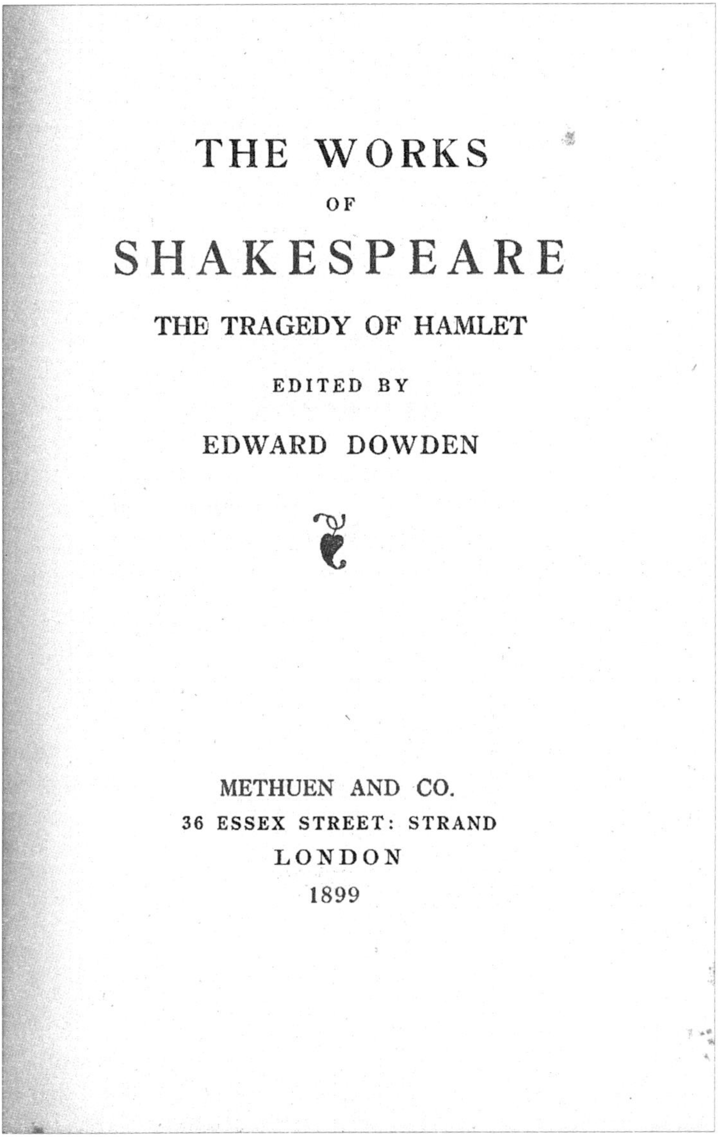

THE WORKS

OF

SHAKESPEARE

THE TRAGEDY OF HAMLET

EDITED BY

EDWARD DOWDEN

METHUEN AND CO.
36 ESSEX STREET: STRAND
LONDON
1899

Figure 1 Title-page of the first Arden *Hamlet*

'is all') and the *British Weekly* ('The editor has done his work in a scholarly fashion. The notes are full of instruction, and are evidently the work of one who understands the English language').[3] It would be pleasing to know to which earlier volume the last remark refers – even more pleasing to believe that all the editions which we produce in such profusion today might deserve the same accolade.

To characterize the first series of the Arden edition in such a thumbnail fashion is perhaps permissible as a way of reminding ourselves of the great gulf of experience which separates us from the generation of our parents, or grand-parents, or great-grandparents. Who now values a 'critical edition of Shakespeare' for combining its attempt at 'textual criticism' with the physical quality of a book 'to be read by the fireside'? Yet it was the first Arden series that developed many of the features of design and layout best known to us today, when a second and third Arden series have been joined by editions under the imprints of the Oxford and Cambridge University presses whose design owes much to the Arden model. Editing Shakespeare today differs in many ways from the task as it presented itself a hundred years ago at the end of the nineteenth century, but we are still familiar with a page on which a legible passage of text is followed by a double column of explanatory notes in smaller type, with eye-straining textual apparatus as the filling of the sandwich or, as in the current third Arden edition, at the foot of the page.

～

The plays we call Shakespeare's on the testimony of his contemporaries, and especially of the joint signatories of the dedicatory and prefatory epistles to the First Folio, Shake-speare's long-time colleagues John Heminges and Henry Condell, were first printed within a forty-year period from 1594 to 1634. About half were published before his death in 1616, the balance (all but one) in the 1623 collection, the most sizeable single publication of plays yet undertaken in England. At least 500 copies of the quartos printed before 1623 (more if we include *The Two Noble Kinsmen* (1634)) are known to survive today and the recent census by Anthony West lists 228 copies of the First Folio.[4] These books are the only source of the text of Shakespeare's plays.

The 1623 edition was advertised in 1622 as 'Playes, written by M. *William Shakespeare*, all in one volume, printed by *Isaack Iaggard*, in fol.'[5] and put on sale in November 1623 as 'Mr. WILLIAM SHAKESPEARES COMEDIES, HISTORIES, & TRAGEDIES. Published according to the True Originall Copies. LONDON Printed by Isaac Iaggard, and Ed. Blount'. It is an exceptional book. What makes it so is that it reflects the faith of a publishing consortium in the risky proposition that plays (never a major concern of any London publisher in Shakespeare's lifetime) might repay the almost unprecedented investment in them represented by so large and expensive a volume. It was probably printed in an edition of 750 copies and retailed at prices ranging from 15*s.* unbound to £1 bound in calf.[6] 'Almost unprecedented', of course, because of the 1616 publication of Ben Jonson's *Works* in folio, a book that contains only nine plays but whose significance in changing perceptions of the status of playwriting and playwrights has received its due of attention in recent decades.[7] Ben Jonson had an active hand in his own collection, whereas Shakespeare had been dead for seven years before the Folio was published.

No reprint of the Jonson volume appeared until the posthumous publication of a much enlarged collection in two volumes in 1640, but the Jaggards – William, who died shortly before publication, and his son Isaac – and their partners, Edward Blount, John Smethwick and William Aspley, got it right. The first reprint of their volume was required a mere nine years after publication, and only three years elapsed after the Restoration of Charles II (and of professional theatre in London) before the second reprint appeared (to be boosted in

1664 by a 'Supplement' of seven extra plays attributed to Shakespeare or to 'W.S.', only one of which, *Pericles*, later found its way into the canon of Shakespeare's works). The Fourth Folio of 1685 may have been designed in part to make good the presumed loss of copies of the Third in the Great Fire of 1666.

This brief summary by Peter Blayney indicates the significance of the First Folio.

> Of the 39 plays now accepted as wholly or partly by Shakespeare, 18 have survived *only* because the First Folio was published. Four more would otherwise have survived only in abridged and inferior versions, and at least half the remainder would have survived in versions differing more or less markedly from the texts we know today. It is hardly surprising that the First Folio has been called 'incomparably the most important work in the English language'.[8]

~

Stationers' Hall is an appropriate setting for this lecture, since it reminds us how much the study and editing of Shakespeare in the twentieth century depended upon research into the conditions of printing and publishing in the London of his day. The records of the Stationers' Company have contributed more than any other single source to increased understanding of the printed books on which our knowledge of the plays Shakespeare wrote wholly relies (give or take 147 lines in the manuscript play of *Sir Thomas More*).[9] Those documents include the day-to-day records of the work of the Clerk of the Company; the entries by its members of copies they intended to print, and in which they wished to register their right and licence to do so; the minutes of the quarterly courts which, among other things, adjudicated disputes and imposed penalties on defaulting members; and the records of the binding of apprentices and of the election of officers. All these have contributed to our sense of the world of normal printing and publishing practice within which, among vastly preponderating numbers of other publications, the literary masterpieces of what we now refer to as the early modern period of English literature, plays included, were manufactured as books and put on sale.

The generosity of the Worshipful Company of Stationers and Newspaper Makers has enabled the work of the scholars who have transcribed and published these records, from Edward Arber in the middle of the nineteenth century, to W.W. Greg, Eleanor Boswell, W.A. Jackson and others in the mid-twentieth century, and the late and much missed Don McKenzie in more recent years.[10] The published records are an essential source for all historical study of the printing trade in the sixteenth and seventeenth centuries, including the publication of Shakespeare's plays. Shakespeare's name became familiar to his contemporaries only in the late 1590s. The first play to name him as its author was *Love's Labour's Lost*, published in 1598. Arber noted 'the first time our great poet's name appears in [the Stationers'] Registers' against the order, dated 23 August 1600, to 'stay' publication of *As You Like It*, *Henry V, Much Ado about Nothing* and Jonson's *Every Man in his Humour*.[11]

By the end of the twentieth century, editors of Shakespeare had access to books and resources undreamed of a hundred years earlier. (Of the resources opened up by electronic technology I shall say nothing, beyond wondering at the skill and expertise which allow me to put the whole of the *Oxford English Dictionary* or the complete second series of the Arden Shakespeare supplemented with a small library of essential works of reference into my pocket with the ease of Mark Antony's handling of 'realms and islands'[12]). The books include works of reference which describe the early editions and locate copies of them, notably Sir Walter Greg's *Bibliography of English Printed Drama to the Restoration*[13] and the two editions of the *Short-Title Catalogue of English Books ... 1475–1640*.[14] Detailed analysis of the printing of early editions provided one focus for the twentieth-century study of Shakespeare's text. Charlton Hinman's *The Printing and Proof-Reading of the First Folio of Shakespeare* (1963) and Peter Blayney's *The Texts of 'King Lear' and their Origins*, volume 1: *Nicholas Okes and the First Quarto* (1982), give meticulous accounts of the printing of these two books and stand out for their evocation of the activities of two Jacobean printing houses engaged in the printing of, respectively, a folio and a quarto.[15]

Among the facsimiles used by editors today, Hinman's Norton facsimile of the First Folio, in its 1996 reprint with a new introduction by Blayney, might be described as the first indispensable book for the library of any serious student of Shakespeare.[16] On its first publication, the Norton facsimile was hailed as the first ever edition of '*the* Shakespeare First Folio',[17] a seemingly paradoxical description based on the proposition that no surviving copy of the 1623 volume represents with such fidelity the book as it was intended to be published. The Norton facsimile was based on exhaustive examination of the process of stop-press correction of the Folio, as a result of which Hinman was able to select from the collection in the Folger Shakespeare Library in Washington, DC, copies of all variant pages in their most correct form (that collection is variously credited with seventy-nine or eighty-two copies of the First Folio).[18]

The story of Henry Clay Folger and the obsessive interest in Shakespeare that led him to collect multiple copies of early editions, especially the four folios, and to endow a research library to house them (and the rest of his unrivalled collection of Shakespearean publications and memorabilia) is itself a remarkable episode in twentieth-century Shakespeare studies. Folger was aware that copies of the First Folio differed in their readings as a result of correction at press. By bringing together the largest ever number of copies in one place since 1623 he made possible an exhaustive investigation of those differences.

The investigation depended on the minute comparison of many copies.

Hinman, having worked during the Second World War in aerial reconnaissance, was familiar with techniques for the visual comparison of aerial photographs to detect movement on the ground. One technique involved the superimposition of reflected images of two photographs on a surface on which they are then made to alternate by the simple device of a rapid alternation of light from one to the other. Differences between the photographs projected show up as flickers in the composite image. Adapting this device to the collation, page by page, of over fifty copies of the First Folio, Hinman was able to determine, as he had set out to do, the full extent of variation between those copies of the book resulting from correction of type undertaken during the printing process (the normal last stage of proof-correction in a carefully printed book of the seventeenth century).[19] At the same time, by magnification of the image, he was able to identify hundreds of distinctively damaged or malformed individual pieces of type. Analysis of these enabled him to determine, at a level of detail and with a degree of confidence unattainable by earlier investigators, not only which typesetter had set each page or section of a page but in what order the type for each page had been set, printed off and distributed back into the type-case.

A further result of Hinman's work, made possible by his access to the Folger collection, was to place the printing of the Shakespeare First Folio, published in November 1623, in the context of a detailed account of the work of the printing shop of William and Isaac Jaggard for the previous two years.[20] Later investigators have refined on Hinman's conclusions, especially in respect of the number and shares of the typesetters who worked on the book (ten compositors, at the latest count, as against Hinman's five).[21] Paradoxically, it was this rather than the disappointing discovery that stop-press correction of the Folio was primarily cosmetic and very rarely of interesting

Iuno sings her blessings on you.
Earths increase, foyzon plentie,
Barnes, and Garners, neuer empty.
Vines, with clustring bunches growing,
Plants, wtth goodly burtben bowing:
Spring come to you at the farthest,
In the very end of Haruest.
Scarcity and want shall shun you,
Ceres blessing so is on you.

Fer. This is a most maiesticke vision, and
Harmonious charmingly : may I be bold
To thinke these spirits?

Pro. Spirits,which by mine Art
I haue from their confines call'd to enact
My present fancies.

Fer. Let me liue here euer,
So rare a wondred Father, and a wise
Makes this place Paradise.

Pro. Sweet now, silence :
Iuno and *Ceres* whisper seriousfly,
There's something else to doe : hush, and be mute
Or elfe our spell is mar'd.

Iuno *and* Ceres *whisper,and fend* Iris *on employment.*
*Iris.*You Nimphs cald *Nayades* of ỹ windring brooks,
With your fedg'd crownes,and euer-harmeleffe lookes,
Leaue your crifpe channels, and on this greene-Land
Anfwere your fummons, *Iuno* do's conumand.
Come temperate *Nimphes*, and helpe to celebrate
A Contract of true Loue : be not too late.
Enter Certaine Nimphes.
You Sun-burn'd Sicklemen of Augult weary,
Come hether from the furrow, and be merry,
Make holly day : your Rye-ftraw hats put on,
And thefe frefh Nimphes encounter euery one
In Country footing.

Enter certaine Reapers (properly habited :) they *ioyne with*
the *Nimphes,in a gracefull dance,towards the end wher-*

Pro. Co

Ar. Th
Pro. Sp
Ar. I t
I thought
Leaft I mi
Pro. Sa
Ar. I t
So full of v
For breath
For kiffing
Towards t
At which I
Aduanc'd
As they fm
That Calfe
Tooth'd b
Which ent
I'th' filthy
There dan
Ore-ftune
Pro. Th
Thy fhape
The trump
For ftale to
Pro. A
Nurture ca
Humanely
And, as wi
So his min
Euen to ro
Enter Ar
*Calib
Cal. Pra
not heare a
St. Mo
Ha done

textual consequence that constituted the most important aspect of Hinman's investigation. The story of the printing of the First Folio has '*alarums and excursions*' in plenty. It tells of extended delay in acquiring the right to reprint Shakespeare's most popular history plays; of how nearly either *Troilus and Cressida* or *Timon of Athens* was omitted (Blayney was later to show that early copies in fact went on sale without *Troilus*[22]); and of the apprentice compositor whose employment on the tragedies, *Hamlet*, *Othello* and *King Lear*, in particular, contributed to the 'editorial problem in Shakespeare'.[23] But I am getting ahead of my narrative.

∽

At the start of the twentieth century one aim of the 'New Bibliographers', W.W. Greg, R.B. McKerrow and their colleague A.W. Pollard, was to improve standards and methods in the editing of early modern English texts, especially plays. Aspects of the editorial practice of the 1890s and the Edwardian years that particularly provoked the rebukes of Greg in his reviews included inaccuracy, inconsistency and choice of the wrong textual basis for an edition. All these could be improved by a fuller understanding of the printing process that had brought a text into the state in which it survived. To make right choices, it was necessary to know what early editions of a play survived, where copies were to be found and what the condition of those copies was. Other important questions were: what was the relation to each other of the surviving editions – in particular, did any later edition offer alterations or augmentation of the text that might be authoritative, or were later editions merely derivative reprints? What evidence could the surviving copies offer about the printing (notably the typesetting and machining and any correction at press, as reflected in variant states of the relevant formes of type)? Was such correction perfunctory or careful? Might its agents have included the author?

These were questions worth asking. When applied to Shakespeare they challenged an orthodoxy assumed in Dowden's textual comments on his *Hamlet*, and voiced by E.K. Chambers in his 1924 British Academy lecture on 'The Disintegration of Shakespeare'. Thanking J.M. Robertson and 'Mr. Dover Wilson' for their questioning of received opinion about the authorship of Shakespeare (and for giving him the occasion to reassert the conventional view), Chambers reflected that 'We had come to think that all the critical questions about Shakespeare were disposed of; the biographical facts and even a little more than the facts chronicled, the canon and the apocrypha fixed, the chronological order determined, the text established; that there was not much left to be done with Shakespeare, except perhaps read him'.[24]

The aim of an edition of Shakespeare that would improve on the texts in the respected Cambridge edition by W.G. Clark, J. Glover and W.A. Wright and published in the 1860s (which may be described as the culminating achievement of the eighteenth-century tradition of eclectic editing of Shakespeare) was not central to the work of all the New Bibliographers.[25] However, the publication of a critical old-spelling edition of his plays, based on a full understanding of the printed evidence can be seen as an underlying ambition in Pollard's *Shakespeare Folios and Quartos*[26] and the *Census of Shakespeare's Plays in Quarto*[27] he published in collaboration with Henrietta C. Bartlett. The same objective is also implicit in Greg's editions of *Henslowe's Diary*[28] and of plays surviving in manuscript, notably (in 1911) *The Book of Sir Thomas More*,[29] with its three pages in a hand soon to be famous as Hand D – the nearest thing to a plausible Shakespearean dramatic manuscript that anyone had yet come up with. The desired critical old-spelling edition of Shakespeare became a more explicit aim in Greg's *The Editorial Problem in Shakespeare* (1942) and *The Shakespeare First Folio* (1955) and of course in McKerrow's own *Prolegomena for the Oxford*

Shakespeare (1939), published the year before his death.[30] This was to be the only part of his critical old-spelling edition, commissioned by the Clarendon Press on the strength of McKerrow's edition of the works of Thomas Nashe,[31] to get beyond proof stage.

While the first Arden edition neared completion and an Oxford edition in original spelling began to be envisaged, the initiative was seized by the Cambridge University Press. From the first energetic espousal of bibliographical methods and ideas by John Dover Wilson in the 1920s, in the volumes of the New Shakespeare (the red-jacketed series familiar to some of us as the 'Cambridge Shakespeare'[32]), the enthusiasm generated by the ideas of Greg, Pollard and McKerrow was to breathe fresh life into the editing of Shakespeare.

◊

The achievements of three generations of New Bibliographers are hard to overestimate. To them the present generation of editors of Shakespeare and the dramatists of his time owe their access to reliable catalogues of the publications of the period, reliable and carefully edited facsimiles of the most important editions of Shakespeare (publications of the greatest importance at a time when the originals themselves are the closely guarded treasures of a few major libraries and collections and are not accessible for handling without serious cause) and a great deal of valuable information about the printing and publishing trade of the time. Editors can now speak with confidence of the printing of the play they are editing and can offer informed conjectures about the kind of manuscript it may have been printed from (although such speculation remains among the more contentious aspects of the New Bibliographical project).

With the deaths of the first generation of New Bibliographers, the task of preparing the 'critical old-spelling edition' moved to their disciples and successors. In England,

Alice Walker took on the mantle of editor for the still-projected old-spelling Oxford Shakespeare, while the tireless energies of Fredson Bowers in Charlottesville, Virginia, extended discussion of the textual basis for a critical edition of Shakespeare to several further volumes of prolegomena for another old-spelling edition which was never to reach fruition.[33] Among the reasons for the non-completion of Alice Walker's Oxford Shakespeare was the editor's growing conviction, as she worked on the early volumes and on her study of *Textual Problems of the First Folio* (1953),[34] that the presentation of Shakespeare to modern users in the orthography of the early editions was intolerable and that the job of an editor, though it must entail the most scrupulous attention to those editions and the fullest understanding of their relation to each other, must also be to cater for non-specialist readers. This, she concluded, could best be done by supplying them with texts that used the intelligible orthographic conventions of their own day, and discouraged the mistaken supposition that in reading the inconsistent spelling and punctuation variously introduced by the compositors of the quartos and the First Folio they were communing with the spirit of Shakespeare.

In the 1970s the Oxford University Press took the bold step of setting up a Shakespeare Department and engaging Stanley Wells (already an experienced editor of Shakespeare) as editor in chief of the long-awaited Oxford Shakespeare. By 1987 Professor Wells and his team, Gary Taylor, John Jowett and William Montgomery, had completed not one Oxford Shakespeare but two, one in modernized spelling, the other in the orthography of the early editions, and their own volume of textual commentary – at last an epilogue rather than a further set of prolegomena – in *William Shakespeare: A Textual Companion*, a 671-page volume comparable in size to the two editions themselves.[35] Just as the Cambridge Shakespeare of the 1860s brought to a suitably comprehensive conclusion the work of editors from the previous century and a half, the Oxford Shakespeare can be seen as the culminating work of the New Bibliographical period in the editing of Shakespeare. This characterization is confirmed by the thoroughness with which the editors engaged with such matters as the early printing and transmission of the text. Readers can find in the *Textual Companion* a responsible synthesis of the state of play as regards, say, press variants, or the division of typesetting between compositors, or the order in which the sheets of a Folio play were printed, as well as a fair, though concise, record of the editorial tradition as it affects truly disputed readings. In many ways, and especially in its thoroughness, the Oxford Shakespeare embodies the ideal, so often voiced by Bowers, of a 'definitive' edition of Shakespeare, though its textual assumptions differ widely from his. But, by a paradox of timing, it was completed and published at a time when that ideal began to be redefined as a mirage. It is the honest claim of its editors that the Oxford Shakespeare should be regarded as what the passing years will undoubtedly reveal it to be, an edition of Shakespeare of its age rather than for all time, an edition which has boldly challenged many conventional views of the texts (both in their readings and their layout), the titles of some plays,[36] the chronology of composition and the canon. Above all it attempts to give a clear sense of the various nature of the surviving materials and of the continuing openness of many questions relating to them.

The decision of the Oxford editors to present their text in two forms, the one fully modernized, the other conforming to the spelling and punctuation of the early editions on which it was based, was pondered and careful. The process of modernization was itself the topic of a serious contribution to a wider and older debate about how dramatic texts of the early modern period might be best presented to twentieth-century users. Stanley Wells published his conclusions in one of the subsidiary volumes generated by the Oxford edition. His position was extreme: modernization must be thorough or be nothing worth.[37] Users of the Oxford Shakespeare may have been startled by an *As You Like It* set in the forest of 'Ardenne' rather than Arden, but they have also been spared the unreasoned sprinkle of original spellings characteristic of modernized editions in the middle of the century (such as 'murther' for 'murder', or 'vild' for 'vile'). The retention on principle of a number of spellings deemed 'Shakespearean' is among the few discordant notes in G. Blakemore Evans's admirable *Riverside Shakespeare* (1974).[38] Radical modernization does, however, produce its own difficulties. These can be acute, for instance with foreign names, especially French ones: 'Orléans', 'Rouen' or 'Marseille' lose the metrical value of the First Folio's 'Orleans' (pronounced 'Orleens'), 'Roan' or 'Marcellus' and additionally suggest a communitarian acceptance of foreigners and their language not habitual in the popular theatre of the 1590s. But if thorough modernization has its awkward aspects it also has the sanction of custom. Though the concept of modernizing may have been unknown to the period before 1660, the practice of regularization of spelling was well under way before the printing of the Folio in 1623, each reprint generally tending towards a more uniform orthography than its exemplar.

'Original spelling' too has disadvantages. To read it easily, and to make sense of 'original' punctuation, requires practice and experience, and preferably some formal awareness of its basis (helpfully supplied in the 'original-spelling' Oxford volume by Vivian Salmon[39]). Furthermore, the orthographic forms in the early editions owe as much (if not more) to the habits of the individual compositor and his adjustment of spelling in order to produce a tight line of type as they do to the orthography of his copy. To print modern editions in 'old spelling' is the most scrupulous way of representing the linguistic detail of the text edited (and much effort by the New

Bibliographers went into devising procedures for retaining an orthography based on the right 'copy-text', the edition identified as standing closest to an authorial manuscript[40]). Particular plays have been published in scholarly and usable old-spelling editions, notably *Romeo and Juliet*, edited by George Walton Williams,[41] but even such an edition involves the uneasy step – if the edited text is to be more than a type facsimile – of 'fake-antiquing' that text where it incorporates editorial emendations or readings from other sources. To divorce the spelling of a printed text from the constraints of lining and page layout that were among its formative conditions is, in any event, to present readers with much insignificant detail whose *raison d'être* is concealed by modern typography and layout. Only in the original, or in a facsimile of that original, can the sense of 'old spelling' be fully conveyed to the reader and its apparent arbitrariness explained by the constraints that shaped it.

On the lower-ground level of the new British Library hangs a painting of a book-filled library with three recessed alcoves. As you approach it, the skilful *trompe l'œil* technique of the painting – the 'receding' parts of which are in fact painted in reverse perspective on projecting surfaces – causes the alcoves to shift and slide, upsetting your initial sense of what you are seeing. This painting, by Patrick Hughes, is called *Paradoxymoron*. It may serve as a fit emblem of Shakespearean editing in our time, in particular of the Oxford Shakespeare. In one view, this is a monumental and authoritative publication, comprising three large volumes and incorporating the fruits of a century of significant research into the nature and status of the printed books on which our knowledge of Shakespeare must continue to depend (and it doesn't even have the projected fourth volume of commentary); in another view, it is a work of remarkable, even self-effacing modesty, which concedes that it will be superseded and offers itself as a merely provisional answer, though a remarkably full and thorough one, to a series of questions which will continue to be asked. The two views are incompatible, and both are true.

⁓

So far I have discussed the study of Shakespeare's text as if it were primarily a technical and material study of the books in which that text has been preserved. But the sanction for such work must lie in the uses that can be made of it. Briefly, these are the increase in confidence that we can gain from being able to rule out fanciful explanations or unsupported hypotheses when we engage in the business of editing Shakespeare. The study of the early editions matters because those editions are the carriers of the words and because that study reduces the area of speculation in our attempt to make sense of those words in the form in which they have survived.

What is it that editors aim to do with the text of their author? Is their role that of archivists, or picture restorers, or collaborators, or even literary executors? How far should their activities extend, beyond presenting the text as accurately as possible in the chosen conventions, towards mediating that text to readers or actors? And how far might that mediation go towards interpretation of the 'work' implicit in the 'text'? Such mediation easily entails engagement with the stated or assumed intentions of the author. 'Authorial intentions' are assumed to inhere in the words of the text by some critics, who accordingly hold as suspect, if not merely a convenient fiction, any claim by editors to special insight into them.[42] Editors are castigated for delusions of power in imagining themselves able to recover the idealized 'single golden authorial manuscript' incorporating an author's final intentions.[43]

Such alleged delusions have been a notable target of materialist critics of the New Bibliographers.[44] Their attacks are given to quoting claims like that of Fredson Bowers to lift the 'veil of print' and reveal the authorial text beneath. That this image clearly inflates the capacity of editorial and bibliographic skill has made it vulnerable to deflating scepticism: behind the 'veil of print' lies a blank page. Bibliographical analysis may aspire to the role of 'the science of discovering error in texts' (in A.E. Housman's famous formulation), but it cannot aspire to that of the answering 'art of removing it'.[45] The lost copy manuscript behind a printed book must remain just that – a lost manuscript.

However, no careful editor of a printed text is going to remain without some conjectural knowledge, especially in matters of detail, of the imagined manuscript from which it was printed. In the case of plays, the misprinting of names will suggest the graphic forms which could have been misread, while the placing of stage directions or the mislining of speech prefixes will easily evoke physical features of what the compositor must have had before his eyes. That the First Folio text of *Othello* was printed from a manuscript transcript rather than from a marked-up copy of the quarto printed in the previous year is argued on several grounds, among them the unlikelihood that even an apprentice compositor would change unfamiliar words that were intelligibly spelt in the quarto – such as '*Antropophague*' for Q's '*Anthropophagie*' (and John Leason, the inexperienced typesetter dubbed 'Compositor E' by Charlton Hinman, set a substantial portion of *Othello*, including the famous speech of Othello to the Duke and Senate).[46]

In the case of the early editions of Shakespeare's plays, it is by now tolerably clear which are reprints of earlier editions and which must have been printed from manuscript copy (though hypotheses about the nature of that copy for a particular play continue to waver between the optimistic pole of authorial manuscripts and the more sober likelihood, at least for the First Folio, of transcripts made for the printer expressly for printing purposes). Mystification about lost printer's-copy manuscripts will no doubt continue to diminish as closer scholarly attention is devoted to the printer's-copy manuscripts that have survived (no plays among them).[47] A good start was made by Peter Blayney in his monograph on the printer Nicholas Okes. In it he considers two manuscripts used as printer's copy in Okes's shop. One is no more than a title-page, the other the text of Sir Anthony Sherley's *Relation of his Travels in Persia*, which either itself served as copy or was the immediate source of a transcript which did. The Sherley manuscript reveals no more about the 'author's intentions' than to represent his text in places more accurately than does the section of the 1613 printed edition of the book produced in Okes's printing-house. Blayney points out that these are the only two surviving manuscripts yet identified as having been used in the shop of any of the twelve printers who printed Shakespeare's plays 'from manuscript copy (of widely varying authority)'.[48]

∽

Twenty-six of Shakespeare's plays survive in a single version, printed either as a separate quarto or in the First Folio. For the plays in question, all later editions are essentially reprints, though these, especially the reprints in the Folio of plays previously printed in quarto, can add material of certain or probable authenticity, such as the deposition scene in *Richard II* or the fly-killing episode in *Titus Andronicus*. They may also introduce interesting variation in stage directions, perhaps reflecting the staging current about 1620. The remaining twelve plays survive in at least two editions that must have been printed from substantially divergent manuscript sources. One group of six plays offers texts of strikingly different length, the earlier in date of publication sometimes not much more than half the length of its successor. The shorter texts of these plays were cast by twentieth-century scholarship in the role of textual whipping-boys by general adoption of the morally loaded label of 'bad' quartos attached to some of them by Pollard in 1909.[49] Recent scholarship has been directed at achieving a more dispassionate estimate, and attempts to re-label them range from the neutral 'short' to Ann Thompson's politically correct 'textually challenged' quartos.[50] I shall return to them in my second lecture.

For six other plays, however, the variant early editions show no such instantly perceptible or radical differences and they have resisted sustained attempts to categorize them as 'good' or 'bad'. They are the focus of what has come to be seen as 'the textual problem in Shakespeare' and they have been more variously edited in the twentieth century than the rest. They are *Richard III* (Q 1597 and F), *King Henry IV, part 2* (Q 1600 and F), *King Lear* (Q 1608 and F), *Troilus and Cressida* (Q 1609 and F) and *Othello* (Q 1622 and F). The sixth play, *Hamlet*, is the most complex of all, as it exists in two versions of high authority, the second quarto of 1604/5 and the Folio, but also in the 'short' first quarto of 1603.

There have been three main ways of editing these plays. The first is the eclectic way, which consists of using the two texts (and in parts of *Hamlet* all three) as ingredients from which to mix the text that best satisfies the aesthetic criteria and critical understanding of the editor, and which were most consistent with his sense of what constitutes 'Shakespeare' (a consideration which allows for rejection as inauthentic of whatever displeases him). The earliest edition to present any form of eclectic text is the second quarto of *Othello* (1630), which incorporates Folio readings into its reprint of the first quarto.

The second way, characteristic of much editing from the 1930s to the present, might be described as 'controlled eclecticism'. Notable examples are to be found in the work of John Dover Wilson and his collaborators for the New Shakespeare, his former student G.I. Duthie for *King Lear* (1960) and Alice Walker, who collaborated with Wilson in editing *Othello* (1957) and also edited *Troilus and Cressida* (1957).[51] One early edition was given primacy in terms of its assumed proximity to an authorial manuscript and therefore superior embodiment of authorial intentions. The chosen text was then edited on eclectic lines, incorporating from the parallel text readings that could reasonably be seen as correcting, or even merely improving it, but with the control of a textual theory that gave precedence to that text in places where editorial adjudication of variants had nothing else to guide it. This proved a flexible and in many ways satisfactory procedure (and it continues to flourish). It ran into difficulty in several areas, among them incompatible staging demands and the absence from the later text of passages which might be seen as theatrical cuts, two categories of variant which offer no possibility of conflation. Dover Wilson's edition of *Hamlet* on the basis of Q2 (1934, revised for successive reprints up to the 1950s) was a pioneering example of this method; Harold Jenkins's 1982 edition of the same play for the second Arden series was its magisterial fulfilment.

A third approach to the editing of the six textually problematic plays has been increasingly in evidence in recent years. It stems from two major developments in textual theory in the 1970s and 1980s, one specific to Shakespeare, the other of wider bearing.

In 1978, Michael Warren proposed that the two texts of *King Lear* constituted, not more or less satisfactory printings of the text of a single play which could be largely reconstructed by eclectic use of both of them (the editorial practice familiar since the 1730s, when Lewis Theobald first constructed such a text[52]), but rather two phases in the evolution of that play, which must therefore be treated as distinct versions, not susceptible of conflation into a single, bigger and better *King Lear*.[53] The idea was not unprecedented, but the rigour with which Warren and others now pursued it was.[54] Warren's own contribution culminated in the publication, in 1989, of *The Complete 'King Lear', 1608–1623*, a collection of scrupulously prepared photographic facsimiles of the first and second quartos and the Folio text of the play.[55] The facsimile included all the many stop-press variants known to exist in copies of the first quarto and the Folio. The second quarto of 1619 was included because of its use in preparation of printer's copy for the Folio. *King Lear* stood revealed (in the few institutional libraries that could afford it) *un*edited – and future editors were supplied with the materials they would need for whatever new forms of text they might devise. Warren's service to future students of *King Lear* was very great, but by demonstrating his view that *King Lear* could not be edited he scored what, in the eyes of other potential users, might look dangerously like an own goal. The Oxford editors, persuaded by Warren's argument and its amplification by other scholars, printed two *King Lears*, a 1608 *History of King Lear* from the quarto and a revised *Tragedy of King Lear* from the Folio.[56]

While Warren's views on *King Lear* were being hotly debated, a broader attack on the principles of editing theorized by Greg and McKerrow, and exemplified in the practice of Fredson Bowers in his editions of the plays of Thomas Dekker and 'Beaumont and Fletcher', was mounted by Bowers's successor at the University of Virginia, Jerome McGann. McGann's *Critique of Modern Textual Criticism* (1983) has become an inevitable point of departure for discussion of editorial theory.[57] His topics, announced in the headings of his chapters, include 'Final Authorial Intentions', 'The Problem of Literary Authority', 'Modernized Editions and the Theory of Textual Criticism'. Shakespeare is not among his primary concerns, except in so far as his works, an important site of much earlier twentieth-century theorizing, bear on the issues he discusses. His general conclusions none the less have an obvious bearing on the editing of Shakespeare, especially of the six 'double-text' plays.

> Faced with the existence of multiple legitimate options, the critical editor should not seek to impose upon them a system which pretends

to distinguish one, ideal eclectic text. Rather, he must come to a judgment about which of the legitimate texts to choose given the demands which are made upon the work from the following quarters: (a) the current state of textual criticism in general, both as to theory and as to practice; (b) the current understanding of the textual history of the work in question, including its composition, production, reproduction, and reception histories; (c) the deficiencies which current critical practice has served to promote and (finally) reveal in the received texts; (d) the purposes of the critical edition's text, both immediate and projected.[58]

Reactions to such new textual thinking have been various, but it has had a visible and immediate effect on the editing of Shakespeare. *King Lear* can now be read in several editions that present both the quarto and Folio texts, either successively, or in parallel on facing pages, or in separate volumes. Three editors of *Hamlet* have chosen to base their text on the later, and slightly shorter, Folio rather than on the second quarto; two of them have gone to the length of relegating passages omitted from the Folio to an appendix of 'additional passages from Q2'.[59] The effect of these operations on interpretation can be at once appreciated by reference to the two well-known film versions of *Hamlet* directed by Laurence Olivier and by Kenneth Branagh.[60] Olivier's 'tragedy of a man who could not make up his mind' hinged on lines (from Hamlet's speech to Horatio as he waits for the Ghost to appear) which he used as an epigraph for the film (though in a cut and adapted text unknown to editors of Shakespeare):

> So, oft it chances in particular men
> That through some vicious mole of nature in them,
> By the o'ergrowth of some complexion,
> Oft breaking down the pales and forts of reason,
> Or by some habit grown too much – that these men,
> Carrying, I say, the stamp of one defect,
> Their virtues else – be they as pure as grace,

> Shall in the general censure take corruption
> From that particular fault.[61]

Branagh's film reaches an almost operatic climax before a late intermission with the last of Hamlet's famous soliloquies, 'How all occasions do inform against me, / And spur my dull revenge', while the distant troops of Fortinbras march on through a winter landscape to their absurd war.[62] Readers of *Hamlet* in the Oxford *Complete Works* will seek in vain for these famous speeches in the text – both are relegated to the Appendix. Several of McGann's criteria have clearly been adhered to in these editions: certainly no attempt has been made to foist on the unsuspecting reader a single 'ideal eclectic text' – but the editorial decision taken pays little attention to the 'reception' of a play whose familiar text over several centuries has included these speeches and it may leave in some doubt 'the purposes of the critical edition's text, both immediate and projected' if those purposes might include provision of texts for performance.

So far three of these textually difficult plays have been published in the third Arden series: *Othello,* edited by E.A.J. Honigmann; *King Lear,* edited by R.A. Foakes (1997); and *Troilus and Cressida,* edited by D.M. Bevington (1998). The general editorial policy of the series is to let editors make their own choice of 'basic text' and of how to present that text to readers. It would in any event have been presumption in the highest degree on the part of the present General Editors to attempt to impose an overall policy on three of the most skilled and experienced editors of Shakespeare in their generation.

Honigmann (whose publications on the subject, from *The Stability of Shakespeare's Text* (1965) onwards, have played a crucial role in shaking earlier editorial aspirations after the 'definitive' text and who has strongly advocated the view that the Folio texts of *Othello* and *King Lear* should be seen as revised versions of the earlier quarto texts) undertook a fresh thorough study of the early editions of *Othello*, published in 1996 as *The Texts of 'Othello' and Shakespearian Revision*. He argued that the printer's copy for the Folio was a transcript by Ralph Crane, the legal scrivener first identified in the 1920s by F.P. Wilson[63] and now recognized as the interventionist transcriber of the copy manuscripts by Jaggard's compositors for at least five of the Folio comedies.[64] Recognizing that many of the deficiencies of the folio text can be (and have been) supplied from the quarto, Honigmann produced a text based on F, but one which accepted more quarto readings than most eclectic editions of *Othello*.

Foakes made a more radical decision about *King Lear*. Seeing the publication of parallel or multiple texts as wasteful of paper and of the reader's time and effort, he produced an innovative edited text, based largely on the readings of the Folio, where the two texts run parallel, but which also included all the additional matter, from single words to a whole scene, which appears in only one or other of the early editions. Where earlier editors have selected among these readings (and have usually omitted many words and phrases unique to the quarto), Foakes's text not only includes them all but indicates exactly where they are by the use of superscript Q and F at the beginning and end of each. This method has not won universal approval, but it forces on the reader's attention the extent to which the familiar 'conflated' *King Lear* is an editorial construct, and it provokes thought about the differing quality of the matter unique to each of the early editions. Where parallel- or double-text editions of Q and F *Lear* take their stand upon the differences of shape and verbal detail between the two, including the Folio's cutting of 300 lines and its introduction of act divisions, Foakes's method stresses instead the extent to which the two 'versions' correspond with each other (despite verbal variants, which are recorded in the conventional textual footnotes). This way

If I would stand against thee, would the reposal
Of any trust, virtue or worth in thee
Make thy words faithed? No, what I should deny,   70
As this I would, ^Qay,^Q though thou didst produce
My very character, I'd turn it all
To thy suggestion, plot and damned practice;
And thou must make a dullard of the world
If they not thought the profits of my death   75
Were very pregnant and potential spurs
To make thee seek it.'   ^F*Tucket within.*^F
GLOUCESTER   ^FO^F strange and fastened villain,
Would he deny his letter, ^Fsaid he?^F ^QI never got him.^Q
Hark, the Duke's trumpets; I know not why he comes.
All ports I'll bar, the villain shall not scape;   80
The Duke must grant me that. Besides, his picture
I will send far and near, that all the kingdom

---

68 **I would** I were to
68–9 **would the . . . worth** would the placing of any trust (as by your father), or would any virtue or merit
70 **faithed** believed
70–7 **No . . . it** With an irony of which Gloucester remains unaware, Edmund attributes to Edgar what is true of himself.
72 **character** handwriting, as at 1.2.62
73 **damned** damnèd
   *practice treacherous scheming. Q has 'pretence', meaning purpose or aim, as at *Mac* 2.3.131.
74 **make . . . world** suppose people to be stupid
75 **not thought** did not think
76 ***pregnant . . . spurs** compelling and powerful incentives. F has 'spirits', which would oddly introduce the notion of evil spirits here, and which I think is a corruption, perhaps by attraction from *spirits*, 53, and *profits*, 75. Sisson, Ard² and Cam² retain F, but

their reasons are more ingenious than convincing.
77 SD *Tucket* a flourish played on a trumpet, here recognized as Cornwall's signature notes
   strange and fastened unnatural (as opposed to *natural*, 84) and determined
78 ***I . . . him** Q only (*got* = begot). F has 'said he?' (referring to 70–1), leaving a short line, possibly marking a pause as Gloucester notices the trumpet sound; but, as Duthie argued, this phrase could be an addition, clarifying the connection with 70–1, not a substitution, even though, with 'I never got him', it makes an irregular long line. Gloucester's denial that he is Edgar's father here matches Lear disclaiming his kinship with Cordelia at 1.1.114–17.
80 **ports** gates of towns, or seaports, or perhaps both
81 **picture** description

---

68 would the reposal] *F*; could the repouse *Q*   70 I should] *Q*; should I *F*   73 practice] *F*; pretence *Q*   76 spurs] *Q*; spirits *F*   77 O strange] *F*; Strong *Q*   79 why] *Q*; wher *F*

Figure 3 Page from the Arden third series edition of *King Lear*, Act 2, scene 1, showing the use of the Q and F superscripts

of presenting the text opens the question whether 'revision theory' may not have tended to overstate its case and to suggest a more radical divergence of structure and purport between quarto and Folio *King Lear* than is in fact to be found, except in a few well-known and important passages (in particular at the beginning and end of the play, but including the Folio's removal of the 'mock trial' of Goneril and Regan by mad Lear from 3.6).

Bevington, after considering the option of printing parallel texts of the quarto and Folio *Troilus and Cressida*, came to conclusions similar to those of Honigmann about *Othello* and produced a Folio-based eclectic text that adopts some quarto readings as preferable and offers a thorough collation of all other Q/F variants. In each of these editions the choice of the Folio as providing the 'basic text' assumes that its readings include identifiable and acceptable corrections of errors in the earlier published quarto.

The one Arden 3 edition that will not follow the plan of controlled eclecticism is *Hamlet*. Its editors, Ann Thompson and Neil Taylor, will present as the new Arden edition of the play an edited text of the second quarto, with full collation of Folio variants. It will be found in a volume that will include the usual Arden contents in the form of introduction, commentary and appendices. In this *Hamlet* the innovation will be the publication, in a second volume, of modernized edited texts of the first quarto and Folio. The second volume will complement and supplement the first, which will, however, remain self-sufficient as the third 'Arden' *Hamlet*.[65]

Where current editorial theory properly lays emphasis on the material state and cultural contexts of the surviving texts, and recent investigation of Shakespeare's texts has reversed earlier optimistic visions of plays printed directly from manuscripts in Shakespeare's own hand and thus affording access to the Bard in action, the needs of users, as McGann properly recognized, will continue to dictate the practicalities of the editing of Shakespeare's plays. A few recent exponents of the extreme theoretical view that editing is an impossible, or even a theoretically improper, activity have found themselves, as contracted editors for current series, in a deeply cleft stick. Practicality appears usually to have won – to the benefit of the users of their editions.[66]

Samuel Johnson, writing of the profession of acting in his prologue for the opening of the Theatre Royal, Drury Lane, of 1747, gave David Garrick the following couplets to speak.

> Ah! Let not Censure term our fate our choice,
> The stage but echoes back the public voice;
> The drama's laws, the drama's patrons give,
> For we that live to please, must please to live.[67]

Mutatis mutandis, editors of Shakespeare must remember that *their* patrons are the actors, students, teachers and others who will buy their editions, and that 'bookish theoric' must of necessity be balanced against the constraints of 'practice'. But I must beware, as I slip into quoting Iago, of the practical editor's envy of the theorist's freedom of speculation.[68]

There is no ideal text of Shakespeare. No single edition will supply the needs of the full range of likely users. For some users, the originals, or the well-edited facsimiles that may serve many of their practical purposes and prevent their over-use, are what is required; for others, a carefully modernized version of a responsible and accurate edited text which reveals to the reader its character and basis will be more helpful. Indeed, an edition of Shakespeare which presented on opposite pages a carefully prepared facsimile and a fully modernized edited text might cut through some of the clutter of textual apparatus familiar in current editions by allowing readers to see for themselves what the editors had done with the early text on which their own was based. As the facsimile testified to the state of the text, so the modernized text would offer commentary on the detail of the facsimile. The method has been used, with great success, in Stephen Booth's edition of the *Sonnets*, where it was motivated by the editor's wish to comment in detail on verbal ambiguity in the poems.[69] For the single-text plays this method would present no difficulty; in the present editorial climate, it might even be deemed appropriate to follow the two-text editions of *King Lear* with similar treatment of the other two-text plays.

Publishers I have consulted don't like the idea of such an edition, mainly because of its expense. But I may merely reveal my own obsolescence in envisaging as a book a form of edition of Shakespeare's plays already flexibly available on screen to users of the *Arden Shakespeare CD-ROM*, which provides facsimiles of quartos and Folio to accompany the edited texts of the second series of the Arden Shakespeare.[70]

~

To conclude I should like to celebrate the solution, by material bibliography, of a longstanding puzzle about a reading in *The Tempest*, perhaps the last such triumph of the twentieth century. During the betrothal masque presented by Prospero to Ferdinand and Miranda, Ferdinand, having learnt from his future father-in-law that the presenters are indeed, as he had guessed, spirits, exclaims,

> Let me live here ever!
> So rare a wondered father and a wise
> Makes this place paradise.[71]

Alden and Virginia Vaughan, Arden editors of *The Tempest*,[72] discuss the word 'wise', for which Nicholas Rowe in 1709 substituted 'wife', despite the agreement of all four seventeenth-century Folios that the word was 'wise'. To distinguish between 'f' and the long 's' in Jacobean printing is not always easy. In the nineteenth century acceptance of Rowe's reading began to be challenged and 'wise' to be restored, although there was unsubstantiated talk of copies of the First Folio in which the word was 'wife'. In 1978 Jeanne A. Roberts claimed that the original letter was in fact an 'f' that had lost the right section of its crossbar in the course of printing the page.[73] The restoration of 'wife' was by some critics acclaimed, not least by feminists. The Arden editors took the question to Peter Blayney, who magnified 'to the 200th power ... all relevant instances of the key word in the Folger Shakespeare Library's extensive Folio collection. The letter in question appears to be "s" in all instances, including the few that Roberts identified with "f"; blotted ink, not a broken crossbar, encouraged such readings'.[74] There the matter could rest, but the editors cannot resist further speculation. Despite their acceptance of 'wise' as what they now know to be the true reading of the Folio, they also know that the copy for *The Tempest* was transcribed by Ralph Crane, a copyist not immune from error, and that printers too can make mistakes. Accordingly they raise the possibility that Shakespeare may, after all, have written 'wife'. Their doubt appears to stem from the wish (first expressed by Rowe's emendation) that Shakespeare *should* have written 'wife' – a view apparently as acceptable to the eighteenth century as to our own times, but less so to the nineteenth and flatly contradicted by the proven evidence of the only authoritative text of *The Tempest*. Honestly, the editors express their doubt, and by so doing remind their readers that the task of editing is a literary and critical undertaking and that it is undertaken at a particular time and for a particular readership – in our time a readership of strongly feminist sympathies. What, very properly, they have *not* done is to emend the text.

2

STAGE

To speak at the new Globe without speaking about the new Globe would prove me, if not necessarily 'a fool', or 'inconstant', at least 'damnable ingrateful'. But I find myself, in consequence, in what Mrs Quickly would describe as a 'canaries'. For the naked truth is that I have nothing to say about the new Globe and its reconstruction that has not already been much better said by others (present company included).[1]

My escape tactics must be rhetorical.

In the opening section of this lecture, then, I do not intend to tell of the vision, persistence and courage of Sam Wanamaker, to whom we all owe our presence here this evening. His absence from the playhouse of which, like Moses, he was to have no more than a Pisgah sight will continue to be felt, whenever we come to the Globe, by those of us who played any role, however marginal, in the years of wandering in the wilderness. I shall not tell the story of academic conferences and colloquia during those years, in a succession of more and more striking and magnificent offices belonging to Pentagram,[2] where Sam maintained, firmly and immovably, his commitment to the highest degree of historical accuracy recommended by the original evidence – and permitted by the London Fire Service – while the no less lamented Theo Crosby, with benign authority, brought scholarly theatres in the air back to earth with a reminder of the real methods, materials and regulations of construction.

I shall not tell of those exciting months in the spring and summer of 1989, when we all trooped down to Southwark Bridge to see the progress of the dig at the Rose and it gradually dawned on us that the best-documented of the Elizabethan arena playhouses was smaller and less tidy than generations of artists' impressions had led us to expect; that it (and by extension the other London playhouses between the 1570s and the 1640s) was built of rough materials and predated the era of the straight line and the right angle. I shall not elaborate on our confusion in face of the first evidence ever discovered of what a professional playhouse of the 1580s and 1590s was really like. How could it not have occurred to us that the floor of the yard would be raked? Or that a 'tiring-house' need have comprised no more than the section of the surrounding galleries behind the stage?

Nor shall I, finally, recall the wonder of the less numerate, as sharp minds, by extrapolation from the foundations of a single stair tower, debated the size of the second Globe.

My confusion is not at an end, as I cannot even use the name of the new playhouse for my opening gambit. Again I have been scooped. Referring to the title of the collection of essays that they published in 1997, Ronnie Mulryne and Margaret Shewring honestly confront a difficulty about their title.

> The title of the present book, *Shakespeare's Globe Rebuilt*, is in various ways misleading. The playhouse to which it refers is not *Shakespeare's* Globe. The Elizabethan Shakespeare contributed no more than one element to a collaborative enterprise which took in business interests and performance and organisational skills without which his abounding genius could not have found expression. He was not the owner of the Globe, though he shared in its ownership. His plays were not, all of them, written for the Globe, though from 1599 to 1613, the years of the first playhouse of that name, he had something of the character of resident playwright with the company who performed there. Nor has the original Globe been rebuilt. *Shakespeare's Globe Rebuilt* stands as the title for and expression of an unattainable ideal. As a book it is the

record of many years of the most committed academic and practical
scholarship which, despite its scruple, knowledge and industry, has had
to resort in matters large and small to inference and compromise, in
order to ensure the construction of the playhouse which now stands in
Southwark.[3]

Like every other aspect of the new Globe, the researches that
preceded its reconstruction, and that reconstruction itself,
have been fully and handsomely documented in this book,
from which you will learn much more on these and a dozen
other related subjects than I could tell you.

In deciding to revise my title from 'Playhouse' to 'Stage',
I have faced myself with a further inconvenience because the
stage is the area of the Elizabethan playhouses about which we
have the least detailed information. And I am, of course,
mistaken when I use the singular and speak of 'the stage' rather
than 'the stages'. Two of the most important pieces of primary
evidence tell us otherwise. From the surviving contract for
building the Fortune playhouse in Clerkenwell in 1600 we learn
of a large raised stage which we usually assume to have been
rectangular. This is congruous with the famous drawing of the
Swan playhouse discovered in 1888, and the frame of the
Fortune certainly was rectangular, so that the stage may well
have been so too. When the chalky piers of the foundations of
the Rose emerged ten years ago, it was a surprise to discover
that its stage, unlike those of the Swan and perhaps the
Fortune, was not rectangular; that the angles of its 'downstage'
corners were oblique and that the pillars which supported its
stage canopy were set far apart towards its extremities.

Since the completion of the new Globe in 1996–7, we have
had the long-wished-for experience of seeing it in action. That
experience involves several quite distinct levels of response.
First and most striking, to my mind, is the very simple
difference between seeing a play done in a setting where
everything collaborates to help the audience to concentrate on
the performance, and the Globe experience of a theatre in

which there can at times seem to be an opposite conspiracy of endless potential distraction. Planes and (worse) helicopters fly noisily over; there is movement in the audience in the yard; people are fainting in coils in the south-east sector of the first gallery; the sun gets in your eyes – or you have to take cover from a sudden shower; a party in the 'Gentlemen's Room' is having a party and indulging in thoroughly Jacobean attention-seeking foolery. Globe audiences, we deduce, were not captive audiences. Clear sightlines and undisturbed performance were conditions unfamiliar to them, as, I suppose, was confinement to a reserved and numbered place in the auditorium (which can, if you are unlucky and the director has given too little thought to the spectators in the side galleries, leave you without a glimpse of extended passages of the action). But we know from Thomas Platter of Basel that the higher prices at the Elizabethan playhouses were paid to obtain a better view of the action (as well as the opportunity of oneself being seen).[4] The Globe galleries have seating less accommodating than Lavatch's barber's chair, kinder to 'the brawn buttock' than to 'the pin buttock' or 'the quatch buttock' (though cushions are provided).[5] All of this adds up to a critique of modern habits of playgoing and a revelation of the extent to which we have come to accept as normal the passivity which all the evidence tells us was not the manner of Elizabethan paying spectators.

We may have doubts about some architectural features of the building. Was it really quite so large (though there is no place in the auditorium which feels remote from the stage)? Were the stage pillars really so massive? Was the gallery quite so high? But we are larger than they were, so these dimensions, even if on the large side, may be appropriate to the early twenty-first century. Should a rebuilt theatre, to be authentic, allow for such considerations?

More significant than any of these matters of structure and size (though related to them) are the building's acoustic properties. From many positions, these are excellent, unless a pillar stands between you and the actor speaking, but it has been demonstrated that not all voices can sustain the level of energy and projection which seems to be required – and that the attempt to overcome the difficulty by shouting merely compounds it. References from the period suggest that people went to hear plays quite as much as to see them, and that vocal and rhetorical prowess were applauded by the 'auditors' in Elizabethan playhouses in the manner of a modern opera audience. 'If I interpret aright some lines of Michael Drayton's', F.P. Wilson wrote in 1955, 'the burst of applause in a thronged theatre might break out at the end of a well delivered speech: "With Showts and Claps at ev'ry little pawse, / When the proud Round on ev'ry side hath rung."'[6]

~

The new Globe has now staged four of the plays which we believe Shakespeare wrote expressly for its original: a comedy, *As You Like It*, a history, *Henry V,* and two tragedies, *Julius Caesar* and *Antony and Cleopatra*. The first three may have been the first plays he wrote for the Globe. They share a self-conscious concern with theatricality (even more apparent in *Hamlet* the following year) that it may not be fanciful to associate with the opening of the new playhouse in 1599. It will not be my business here to evaluate these productions (I have already reviewed two of them, *Antony and Cleopatra* for the summer issue of *Around the Globe*,[7] and *As You Like It* for *Shakespeare Survey*[8]). It is enough to say that the experience of Shakespeare in 'Shakespeare's Globe' can be, and has been for me, an exhilarating one. We have seen *Antony and Cleopatra* played with few cuts and within three hours. We have been shown how the casting of men in female roles lends sudden prominence and interest to minor roles sometimes under-cast in conventional productions (although we can hardly pretend that this would have been the Elizabethan

Figure 4 *Antony and Cleopatra*, Act 2, Scene 7, at Shakespeare's Globe, Bankside, 1999

experience of cross-dressing). We have delighted in period music on period instruments and in costumes of authentic cut, colour and fabric. Above all we have enjoyed a unique theatrical setting of such warmth and beauty that simply to enter the yard is to step into a world of pleasure. The opportunities offered by the theatre are golden, and after only three years we can see those opportunities increasingly being taken and can look forward to many more happy afternoons and evenings in Southwark, especially when it is made easier of access by the Millennium footbridge.

∼

The Globe experience is new, but it is not unrelated to other experiences of Shakespeare in performance in the second half of the twentieth century. It reopens questions asked in 1968 by the Canadian theatre critic Nathan Cohen, reflecting on a production of Shakespeare at the Festival Theatre in Stratford, Ontario. That theatre, in a tent for its first nine years, then housed in a handsome building with a large open stage designed by Tanya Moseiwitch, was where Tyrone Guthrie developed ideas of staging with which he had first experimented in the Assembly Hall of the Church of Scotland at Edinburgh Festivals in the late 1940s. Cohen's views are summarized by Robert Speaight:

> He noted what no apologia could disguise, that only a third of the audience could at any one time see and hear the actors. The enlarged perspective in which they stood to one another was annulled for the spectator. Moreover the public were embarrassed by the players hurtling down the gangways; a proximity and a kind of quasi-participation, helpful in some cases to comedy, were inimical to tragedy.[9]

Speaight continued:

> when the hypothetical question is put – is this how Shakespeare would have liked to see his plays performed if he were alive today? – one can return only a qualified affirmative. The experiment was abundantly worth making, but it raises as many problems as it solves. It should

not be regarded as the last word on a subject on which the last word can never be spoken. Nevertheless it conveyed a warning which Christopher Plummer passed on to Laurence Olivier: 'You can't lie.' 'My God,' replied Olivier, 'what are we going to do?'[10]

'Is this how Shakespeare would have liked to see his plays performed if he were alive today?' The question is, of course, meaningless. Would he hold a ritual burning of the First Folio and set about writing more new plays? Would he reflect with satisfaction on the success of the minor industry which has been built on his own labours and business acumen? What the question really points to, I suppose, is rather: where are we to find criteria for 'authenticity' in the performance of Shakespeare's plays today?

Among many different approaches to this question, one is certainly the building of appropriate playhouses. The company of which William Shakespeare was a member from 1594 until his death in 1616 owned and acted in four London playhouses. These were James Burbage's Theatre, built in 1576 and taken over by the newly formed Chamberlain's Men in 1594; its neighbour and 'easer' the Curtain, which they rented in 1597–9 during the interim between the closure of the Theatre, when the lease of the land it was built on ran out, and the building of the Globe; then the Globe itself, their main, and indeed only, house from 1599 to 1608; and finally the indoor playhouse in the upper frater of the dissolved Blackfriars monastery. James Burbage had bought this in 1596 and refurbished it as the company's next home after they lost the Theatre, but they were then prevented from using it after Blackfriars householders successfully petitioned against public playing in their area of the City. This theatre finally became available to them in 1608, after the collapse of the children's companies that had occupied it as their tenants between 1600 and 1606. Which London theatres Shakespeare may have acted in before 1594 remains a matter for speculation, though it seems likely that they included the Rose (where *Titus Andronicus* and probably the play we call *King Henry the Sixth, Part 1* – 'harey the vj' to Henslowe – were both performed between the summer of 1592 and the spring of 1594).[11]

But this list of London playhouses suggests too simple a picture of the real life of an Elizabethan and Jacobean acting company, especially the reality of command performances for royal or noble patrons and the reality of touring. The possession of a home base – the first step towards the dominance of English theatrical life by London – was an innovation of the 1570s, and touring would remain a regular activity of the London-based companies well into the 1630s. Shakespeare in his time must have acted, in his own plays and those of others, in dozens of different places and circumstances. They performed at court, in various royal residences; at the houses of noble patrons; in the Great Halls of the Inns of Court (two such performances give us our first glimpses of .*The Comedy of Errors* and *Twelfth Night*[12]) and on tour. Shakespeare's own company may have toured less than some, and for the period from August 1597 until March 1603 it would appear not to have left London, 'evidently happy', in the words of Andrew Gurr, 'to exploit its new and quasi-unique right to remain in London to the full';[13] although the uncertainty about a permanent base in London for the company in 1597–9 may also have imposed some restrictions on its mobility during these years. Besides, it must have been during these years that *Hamlet*, written in 1600, was performed, as the title-page of the first quarto of 1603 tells us, 'in the two Vniuersities of Cambridge and Oxford, and else-where', so that they must have made at least one short tour.

A recent study by Scott McMillin and Sally-Beth MacLean of an earlier company, the Queen's Men, gives a fuller picture than has hitherto been available of that company's many extended tours, from its formation in 1583 until it disappears from view towards the end of the reign of Queen Elizabeth I.[14] They are able to draw on the detailed evidence provided in the eighteen volumes (so far, with as many more to come) of *Records of Early English Drama*, published in Toronto since the 1970s and familiarly known as *REED*.[15] These volumes collect excerpts from archival sources, public and private, that relate to drama in England from its medieval origins to the closure of the theatres in 1642. The information contained in them, including that of earlier investigators, confirms the wide extent of touring and the regularity of the routes followed by the various companies. The Queen's Men are of especial interest in the light of strong arguments presented by McMillin and MacLean support the view that Shakespeare is likely to have been a member of this company before his emergence as a leader of the Chamberlain's Men in 1594. If Shakespeare did belong to the Queen's Men, then their tours could have taken him west as far as Plymouth or north to Carlisle, Newcastle upon Tyne or even Edinburgh, as well as over the company's more regular routes through Kent, East Anglia and the Midlands.

A census by Alan Somerset in 1994 of all the material then available from the files of *REED* revealed that, of over 3,000 records of visits by touring players, only forty-two specifically name the place of performance – information that would usually be too obvious to need recording.[16] But several of those named buildings survive, or have been faithfully restored, thus offering the prospect of sharpened awareness of the different circumstances of playing which the touring players confronted. Seven buildings recorded as playing-places certainly or probably used by the Queen's Men are described in detail by McMillin and MacLean. They range from civic guildhalls in Leicester, Norwich and York to the second-floor room of the Church House in Sherborne, Dorset, and the splendour of the High Great Chamber of Hardwick Hall in Derbyshire; they may perhaps include the Great Halls of

Trinity College, Cambridge, and Christchurch, Oxford. The authors write:

> We may conclude that performance conditions for the Queen's Men, as for other play troupes on tour, were more congenial than has often been assumed. Many, if not most, of their performances would have been indoors, in halls that may have varied in size but would have been comfortably appointed. This was an era of secular building closely related to evolving civic pride, and efforts taken to dignify and maintain the environment of town halls undoubtedly were characteristic of private halls also. ... These provincial 'theatre' spaces were not designed for a uniform purpose, however, and flexibility in adapting plays to differing audiences and varying locations would have been a basic requirement for all touring players. Given the range of locations involved on a tour, they could not have counted on more than minimal furnishings such as scaffolding, hall benches, forms and trestles at all their tour stops, although other props such as house-keeping equipment may have been available to them on site. Our survey of the staging requirements of the Queen's Men's plays ... shows that most of them would have travelled easily, so long as a portable 'canopy' or 'pavilion' was among their properties [to serve as a 'discovery-space'].[17]

~

With these provisos, it still remains important and appropriate to investigate the available evidence about the Chamberlain's Men's London playhouses. On the occasion of this commemorative lecture, the focus must be the first Globe itself. In 1975 Richard Hosley, an influential theatre scholar, pointed out that 'Very little is known about the physical features of the First Globe.'

> We know nothing ... about the Globe stage and tiring-house. In view of this lack of information, I suggest the hypothesis that the stage and tiring-house of the First Globe were generally similar to the stage and tiring-house of the Swan. Thus the Globe would have had a large rectangular stage, a trap door set in the middle of the stage, a tiring-house with two doors opening on the stage, a gallery over the stage divided into boxes, and suspension gear housed within a stage

superstructure consisting partly of the hut we know of from the pictorial sources and partly of a stage cover that may be postulated immediately beneath the hut, the front of the superstructure being supported by posts rising through the stage from the yard below.[18]

His inference that the stage was modelled on the Swan gains some collateral support from the extant builders' contracts for the Fortune and Hope playhouses. Peter Street, builder in 1599 of the Globe, was given instructions, a year later, to equip the Fortune with a stage and tiring-house and

a shadowe or cover over the saide Stadge, which Stadge shalbe placed & sett, as alsoe the stearecases of the saide fframe, in suche sorte as is prefigured in a plott thereof drawen [this plot, alas, has not survived], and which Stadge shall conteine in length Fortie and Three foote of lawfull assize and in breadth to extende to the middle of the yarde of the saide howse; The same Stadge to be paled in belowe with good, stronge and sufficient newe oken bourdes … And the saide Stadge to be in all other proporcions contryved and fashioned like vnto the Stadge of the saide Plaie howse called the Globe.[19]

The Hope contract, in 1613, makes similar reference, for unnoted details, to 'the Plaie house called the Swan in the libertie of Parris garden'.[20]

In the absence of better pictorial and documentary evidence, Hosley turned to the most important surviving body of relevant material – the texts of the plays performed by Shakespeare's company at the Globe between 1599 and 1608 (the necessary cut-off date, as later texts could have been designed for the indoor Blackfriars playhouse).[21] Of the twenty-nine surviving 'First Globe' plays, fifteen are by Shakespeare, the resident 'ordinary poet' (to use the term later applied to poets contracted to particular playing companies which G.E. Bentley thought likely to relate also to Shakespeare's contractual status within his company). They range in date from *As You Like It* (1599) to *Pericles* (1608), including the undatable *Timon of Athens*.

Three more, *Every Man Out of his Humour, Sejanus, his Fall* and *Volpone*, are by Ben Jonson; two, *The Revenger's Tragedy* and *A Yorkshire Tragedy*, as we now believe, by Thomas Middleton; one each by Thomas Dekker (*Satiromastix*), Barnabe Barnes (*The Devil's Charter*) and George Wilkins (*The Miseries of Enforced Marriage*). The remaining five are of unknown or conjectural authorship: *The Tragedy of Thomas, Lord Cromwell* 'by W.S.' and *The London Prodigal* – printed, like *A Yorkshire Tragedy*, as 'by William Shakespeare' – would find their way, with it and *Pericles*, into the *Supplement* to the Third Folio in 1664. The remaining three are *A Larum for London, or The Siege of Antwerp* (a grim anti-Spanish polemic); *The Merry Devil of Edmonton*, among the best-known and best-loved comedies of the early seventeenth century; and *The Fair Maid of Bristol*, a romantic tragicomedy.[22]

Hosley's findings were clear and simple. Twenty plays 'refer in stage directions to two doors'; nine use the 'discovery-space', *The Devil's Charter* nine times, *Cromwell* three and seven others once each. But those seven, and a further twelve, also 'explicitly avoid the device of discovery by calling for carrying on of stage properties or players'. Action '*above*' is required by eleven plays; once each in nine (though the pulpit for the funeral orations in *Julius Caesar* was not regarded by Hosley as being '*above*'[23]), twice in *Every Man Out* and no less than five times in *The Devil's Charter*. Seven plays locate music required as sounding '*within*'; six of these are Shakespeare's, the seventh is *The Devil's Charter*. No stage direction in any play locates musicians '*above*', so that 'we may conclude that the music station was probably "within" the tiring-house at stage level'.[24]

Act divisions, with or without musical interludes, now seen as a feature of performance at the indoor playhouses, are absent from 'some three-quarters of the texts of Globe plays printed before 1609', but increasingly appear after the occupation of the Blackfriars. The exceptions are Jonson's plays, 'probably due ... to Jonson's predilection for neoclassical trappings', as well as *The Revenger's Tragedy* and *The Devil's Charter.* 'We may conclude that before 1609 the Globe plays were probably performed without act intervals, hence probably without inter-act music'.[25]

Suspension gear (for a strappado and a hanging) is required by *A Larum for London*,[26] while it is also probably relevant to the stage direction in *Antony and Cleopatra* (4.15.37 SD), '*They heave Antony aloft to Cleopatra*' – Hosley thinks a chair would have been used to stabilize the flying, dying Antony, but the breeches-buoy used in 1999 at Shakespeare's Globe served very well and captured the mixture of pathos and comedy of the moment. Use of the stage posts as places of concealment may be implied when one character in *A Larum* climbs a tree, or where Roderigo is instructed by Iago to stand in ambush for Cassio 'behind this bulk' (*Othello*, 5.1.1). Finally, 'Four plays require a trap door.' No prizes are offered for identifying two of them as *Hamlet* (for the grave of Ophelia) and *Macbeth* (for the weird sisters' cauldron in 4.1). The third is *A Larum*, where a Jew is first pushed through the trap and then, safely out of sight, stoned to death.[27] The fourth is *The Devil's Charter*, which requires the trap no fewer than three times, for ascents and descents of devils and others, and for dumping murdered bodies in the Tiber.[28] Only *Hamlet* (1.3) and *Antony and Cleopatra* (4.3) make use of the space beneath the stage – for the special auditory effects of the Ghost's injunctions to 'Swear' and the unearthly music that signifies the desertion of Antony by 'the god Hercules'.

While these findings depend to some extent on the accidental survival of plays from what must have been a much larger repertoire, a few inescapable conclusions present themselves. Shakespeare, presumably the most regular writer for the Globe, made very sparing use of its special facilities. Possibly one consideration was the need to write plays that could be easily and effectively transferred to the different conditions of court performance, especially during the all-important and lucrative

Christmas Revels. 'Barnabe Barnes's Globe' was a rather more sensational theatre than 'Shakespeare's'. It pulled out all stops to counter the *longueurs* and flat writing of *The Devil's Charter* – a serio-comic melodrama of the crimes of the Borgias, framed by the compact of Pope Alexander VI with an (inevitably) deceitful devil, which I have always wished to subtitle 'Popes, Poison and Pederasty'. But perhaps Barnes's spectacular staging was merely an overflow of his own fantasy. *The Devil's Charter* was printed in 1607, with proud reference to its royal command performance 'vpon Candlemasse night last' on its title-page and with a note that the printed text was '*more exactly reuewed, corrected, and augmented since by the Author, for the more pleasure and profit of the Reader*'.[29] The Globe could have supplied his staging requirements, but they would presumably have needed modification for performance at court.

∽

After so close a look at the way in which play texts may help us to understand the physical features of the undocumented Globe stage, I now propose to widen the inquiry and say something of other ways in which play texts – specifically some of the texts of Shakespeare's plays – have been interrogated for what they may tell us of performance.

Among the printed texts of the period, one group has been regarded as offering particular insights into stage practice. This group comprises the so-called 'bad' quartos, which, in the case of Shakespeare, can be seen to differ markedly from the alternative versions published in later quartos or in the First Folio. Many different explanations have been put forward to account for the radical divergence of these editions from the 'authorized versions' printed in the First Folio. A.W. Pollard's classification of them as 'bad'[30] reflects the first response of most readers familiar with the longer versions. Are their brevity, their stylistic untidiness and uneasy versification, and their simplification of issues, to be best accounted for by seeing them as rough authorial drafts, as copies scribbled in shorthand by spectators in the pay of grasping stationers, as makeshift versions put together from memory by touring players called on for a sudden performance in the sticks, or as authorized acting abridgements? I can best introduce this question to anyone unfamiliar with them by using the best-known, but sufficiently typical, illustration.

> To be, or not to be, I there's the point,
> To Die, to sleepe, is that all? I all:
> No, to sleepe, to dreame, I mary there it goes,
> For in that dreame of death, when wee awake,
> And borne before an euerlasting Iudge,
> From whence no passenger euer retur'nd,
> The vndiscouered country, at whose sight
> The happy smile, and the accursed damn'd.
> But for this, the ioyfull hope of this,
> Whol'd beare the scornes and flattery of the world,
> Scorned by the right rich, the rich cursed of the poore?[31]

As Shakespeare is my subject, I shall concentrate on the seven Shakespearean 'bad' quartos, merely reminding you that a recent study by Laurie Maguire lists no fewer than forty-one 'suspect texts' of Elizabethan and Jacobean plays.[32] What they are suspected of is deriving from the recollection of an actor or actors rather than from a process of manuscript transcription. The aim of this study was to set up a rigorous inquiry into the hypothesis of 'memorial reconstruction' of play texts by actors. Of the forty-one alleged 'bad quartos' examined, seven are versions of plays by Shakespeare. Deducing that a small minority of printed play texts might indeed be of memorial origin, Dr Maguire found no sufficient grounds for extending this explanation to the remainder. Her small 'memorial' group includes the first (or only) quartos of *The Taming of the Shrew* (called *A Shrew* in the quarto of 1594), *The Merry Wives of Windsor* (1602), *Hamlet* (1603) and

Pericles (1609); while she concludes that the first editions of *King Henry VI, Part 2* (1594) and *Part 3* (1595), *King Henry V* (1600) and *Romeo and Juliet* (1597) may be seen as preserving more or less reliable versions of abridged acting texts of those plays.[33]

Scholarly attention was drawn to these texts in 1910 by W.W. Greg's edition of the quarto text of *The Merry Wives of Windsor* (1602),[34] in which he proposed, on the basis of comparison with the longer Folio version, that the quarto text was a memorial one, compiled by an actor who had played the role of the Host of the Garter. His suggestion was based on the proposition that most of the scenes in which the Host appears correspond more closely with the Folio text than do other parts of the quarto. Subsequent controversy over these 'short' quarto texts has been long and heated, and it shows little sign of abating. It has followed a number of false trails and blind alleys. There is now reasonable consensus on two points: the texts weren't written in shorthand by a concealed copyist in the theatre (no shorthand system known at the time could have produced such good results[35]); and their publication need not necessarily have entailed conscious dishonesty on the part of the publishers, or of the men who supplied them with manuscript copies from which to print the plays.[36] The latter suspicion stems, of course, from the famous claim of Heminges and Condell that the First Folio would supersede 'diuerse stolne and surreptitious copies, maimed, and deformed by the frauds and stealthes of iniurious impostors, that expos'd them'.[37] Attempts have frequently been made to interpret this attack as specific to the 'short' quartos, but it now seems quite as likely that its blanket claim for excellence has a simple commercial aim, to disable all previous quarto publications (including those of which the Folio itself is no more than a lightly edited reprint).

～

Association of the 'short' quartos, or at least the most celebrated of them, *Hamlet* (1603), with the theatre in fact antedates Greg by at least thirty years. In 1881 the actor and producer (or, as we would now say, director) William Poel read photo-lithographic facsimile reprints of the first and second quartos of *Hamlet* published in 1880.[38] He immediately became interested, and on 1 February 1881 he wrote to the leading Shakespearean scholar F.J. Furnivall, who had written forewords for the facsimiles.

> If to the literary student the Quarto of 1604 has the chief interest, I feel sure that to an actor the Quarto of 1603 has an equal interest, because however misrepresented the text may be, the actor cannot help recognizing that the Editor has endeavoured to reproduce the play as *he* saw it represented and therefore in the arrangement of the scenes, the stage directions, the omissions, and the alterations, there is much to guide and instruct him in the stage representation of the play as it appeared in Shakespeare's time. There was so much that was new and interesting to me, from a dramatic point of view, in the first Quarto, that I could not help thinking, if the printer's blunders could be corrected, a performance of the Quarto might be of some interest to students.

Poel's 'Editor' would seem to have been envisaged as a spectator who reported the play. Poel's view of the three texts of *Hamlet* was that the First Folio printed 'the Globe Playhouse acting edition of the play', while the second quarto of 1604/5 (barring printer's errors) gave us 'Shakespeare's perfect work from his own manuscript'.[39] In contrast to Furnivall, who took Q1 to 'represent, or misrepresent, Shakspere's first sketch of his great play',[40] Poel saw it as 'a deliberate tampered version of the Globe Playhouse copy [i.e. the Folio text], reconstructed and compressed with considerable practical knowledge of stage requirements, a knowledge that shows the skill of the actor or stage manager, and not that of the poet or dramatist'.[41] Among notable stage improvements in Q1 he included the placing of 'To be, or not to be' and the nunnery scene before the arrival of Gilderstone and Rossen-craft or the players, and the clear commitment of Queen Gertred to her son's cause in the final acts. That the reporter/editor had seen a performance of the version of *Hamlet* he transcribed was argued by the visual clarity of stage directions such as '*Enter the ghost in his night gowne*' (G2^v) and '*Enter Ofelia playing on a Lute, and her haire downe singing*' (G4^v).

Poel accounted for what he saw as 'Shakespeare's language imperfectly reported' in terms of his own experience as a actor, speaking of:

> those actors' liberties which are so often taken with the author's language; such as the interpolation of exclamations, the 'Ay, father', 'Oh, I have it', 'the better the better' and the repetition of sentences such as 'to a nunnery go, to a nunnery go'. Again we have ... the interpolation of lines in a later scene that should have been spoken in an earlier one, or the introduction of a line from another play where the actor's memory has failed to retain any of the words, an illustration of which occurs in the speech of Corambis (Polonius):
>
> > Such men often prove
> > Great in their words, but little in their love,
>
> when the actor may have been thinking of Viola's words:
>
> > For still we prove
> > Much in our vows but little in our love.
>
> All actors who have served in a stock company, where the playbill has been changed nightly, know how easily these mistakes are made.[42]

On 16 April 1881, less than three months after he wrote to Furnivall, Poel duly staged the first quarto text of *Hamlet*, with himself in the lead and an amateur cast ('to avoid much expense'), 'on the bare, draped platform' of St George's Hall.[43]

The event had a double significance. It was the first time on record that the first quarto of *Hamlet* had been performed; and it was a radical experiment (the first of very many to be conducted by Poel) in simplicity of staging and submission to

Figure 5 A production of Q1 *Hamlet* (c. 1900?) by William Poel, showing Ophelia, played by a boy, mad, with loose hair and lute (from Poel's scrapbook, British Library)

the demands of the text. Robert Speaight, Poel's biographer, rightly identifies the 1881 performance as a significant moment in Shakespearean stage history and as 'the birth of a new idea',[44] from which one main line of theatrical thinking about Shakespeare was to run through the twentieth century. Poel launched a practical, text-based, theatrical inquiry into the staging and acting of Shakespeare which directly opposed and challenged the elaborately pictorial style of production in vogue in the late Victorian years, with its consequences of time-consuming scene changes and heavily cut and adapted texts. His ideas did indeed inspire much dedicated work in the twentieth century, starting with that of Harley Granville Barker.

The 1881 *Hamlet* was not a critical success: a friendly commentator noted that 'the critics had no sympathy with an experiment the nature of which they did not understand'.[45] The level of unsympathetic misunderstanding is expounded by Dutton Cook.

> The attitude of the general audience was one of apathy tinctured by a disposition to deride.... To many the performance was wearisome and depressing; while a strong feeling prevailed that, upon the whole, the experiment was of an absurd and reprehensible sort, involving, as it did necessarily, some degradation of the poet in whose honour it purported to be undertaken.[46]

Punch published a parody, whose targets included Furnivall's habits of emendation, as well as Poel's production and what clearly struck the parodist as Q1's prosiness.

> To be, or not to be? There you are, don'tcherknow!
> To die, to sleep! Is that all? Forty winks?
> To sleep, to dream! Ah, that's about the size of it
> For from that forty winks when we awake
> In the undiscovered cotton-nightcap-country
> From which no passenger ever took a return ticket –
> Why – ah, yes – humphexactly – very much so![47]

Poel and his amateur 'Elizabethan Stage Society' offered an easy butt for humour and satire, but his influence is still alive and he may even, without absurdity, be seen as the 'onlie begetter' of the desire for historical accuracy in the staging of Shakespeare which has led at last to the rebuilding of 'Shakespeare's Globe'.[48]

∼

There has of late, but wherefore I know not, arisen a loud claim for the Shakespearean 'bad' quartos to be rechristened, together with all other first editions of his plays, as 'Shakespeare Originals'. The claim is founded on the twin assumptions that the 'short' texts originated in the theatre and that they are not garbled reports but abridged acting texts. Picking up (unconsciously?) Poel's distinction between the 'actor or stage manager' and the 'poet' (and conveniently forgetting that Shakespeare, whatever may have been his stage-managerial skills, was both poet and actor), the champions of the short texts have gone to the extreme of claiming that they represent, not merely alternative stage versions of the plays in question, but superior ones, quarantined from any elitist notion of 'poetry' or 'literature' but partaking of the wholemeal wholesomeness of anonymous, collaborative 'theatre'. It is true, as Graham Holderness and Bryan Loughrey write in their 'General Introduction' to the 'Shakespeare Originals' series of which they are General Editors, that 'The script', though 'of course, an integral element of drama, ... is by no means the only one' and equally true that 'even in the early modern theatre, dramatic realisation depended not just upon the scriptwriter, but upon actors, entrepreneurs, promptbook keepers, audiences, patrons, etc.; in fact, the entire wide range of professional and institutional interests constituting the theatre industry of the period.'[49]

It is, I suppose, also true that 'institutional interests' haven't written many plays and inescapably true that all that survives of Elizabethan and Jacobean theatre is a collection of those scripts, more in print than in manuscript, a scatter of documentary records and the reinterred remains of the Rose and the Globe. The desire to associate those scripts with theatrical performance is both natural and inevitable, but the nature of that association is likely to remain largely obscure.

Poel's interest in the first quarto of *Hamlet* has been revived in recent decades, which have seen several productions of its version of the play and a mass of critical writing about it, including an anthology of essays edited by Thomas Clayton under the impeccably non-committal title of *The 'Hamlet' First Published: Q1 (1603)*.[50] The essays cover a wide spectrum of views of Q1: advocates range from those who see it as Shakespeare's first draft (Stephen Urkowitz[51]) to proponents of the more orthodox reporting theory (Kathleen Irace[52]). Scott McMillin addresses the question whether grounds do exist for claiming that Q1 has greater claims to 'theatrical' origins than the longer Q2 and F texts. He uses a tool, in part developed by himself, which several recent theatrical researchers have found of great value, the determination of the minimum size of cast required to act a play.[53] His conclusion, that the three texts of *Hamlet* make exactly the same (surprisingly modest) casting demand for eleven players – eight adults and three boys – leads him to conclude that all three texts stand in the same, carefully calculated, relation to performance, and that to dismiss Q2 as a text of poetic rather than theatrical interest is accordingly mistaken and based on a false contrast. Q2, he demonstrates, is designed with exactly the same professional care for the constraints of casting and doubling as the allegedly more 'theatrical' Q1 and F. This need not surprise us: its author was a professional man of the theatre, whose professionalism is nowhere more apparent than in his constant awareness of the constraints of casting and doubling upon the dramaturgy of his plays. 'All three texts' of *Hamlet*, McMillin concludes, 'are imbued with the theatrical'.[54]

If we have advanced since 1881, it is in the wider recognition that we need to be familiar with the *Hamlet* (and *Romeo and Juliet*, and *Merry Wives*, and *Henry V*) 'first published'. In 1995, T.W. Craik's edition of *Henry V* (1995) for the third Arden series printed a slightly reduced facsimile of the first quarto in an appendix. Similar facsimiles have now appeared in the Arden editions of *King Henry VI, part 2* (1999) and *The Merry Wives* (2000). The Malone Society's millennial publication is a full-sized facsimile of the least accessible of the group, *Romeo and Juliet (1597)*.[55] It has recently published *The Taming of A Shrew (1594)*,[56] a quarto which has the odd distinction of being simultaneously the first 'Shakespeare' play to be printed and the earliest adaptation of Shakespeare. The full case for this view can be found in Stephen Miller's modernized edition of *A Shrew*.[57]

For *Hamlet*, the first quarto offers a two-hour performing text, a pared-down, fast-moving revenge play, stronger on action than on introspection. Several revivals since the 1970s have supplied scholars and critics with yet more to write about *Hamlet*. In the Clayton anthology, an interview by Bryan Loughrey with Peter Guinness, who played Hamlet at the Orange Tree, Richmond, in 1985, gives useful insights into the text's value for modern actors. The unfamiliar wording rids the play of 'the clichés that punctuate the more familiar version' (we recall the mythic old lady's comment on emerging from the theatre: 'I didn't know *Hamlet* was so full of quotations').

> the First Quarto ... has an energy and edge that the Folio in all its refinement, particularly its poetic refinement, doesn't have. I'm not saying that one is better than the other; I'm just saying that from an actor's point of view, it was a joy to have that muscularity and directness. If you work on film, you work very hard at reducing the script – the scriptwriter has written too many words, so we can get rid of a few. What you end up with very often is a skeletal version of what the screenplay had to say. I think this is what the First Quarto is like.

It's a skeletal version, but at the same time it's the absolute bare bones, the absolute dynamo behind the play; and that comes singing across, very clearly.[58]

The Orange Tree production was played in the round, in what my memory conjures up as a room of only moderate size above the Orange Tree pub. The high excitement it generated was partly a result of proximity. I was harrowed with fear and wonder by the Ghost, standing just behind me, at shoulder level, for his admonitions to Hamlet. Guinness's Hamlet was older than most, but also tougher and less likeable than any other I can remember. The actors had *un*learnt the more familiar lines with total dedication.

Whether or not Q1 *Hamlet* began life as a 'touring' text (Poel's opinion of the matter), it lent itself to the simple setting of an upper room in a pub. But that it has a 'theatrical' integrity denied to Q2 and F is a romantic fantasy. It is often associated with such mystification of theatre as that of Stephen Urkowitz when he proposes that 'efforts at endowing alternative scripts, whatever their origins, with meaning may lead us to transcendent or at least intense aesthetic experiences', or sets up a surely over-determined, if not just starry-eyed, contrast between 'the essentially irrational' experiences of theatrical performance and 'the deductive linearities of most bibliographical and literary analysis'.[59] We need not be enlightenment rationalists to endorse Samuel Johnson's statement that 'the spectators are always in their senses, and know, from the first act to the last, that the stage is only a stage, and that the players are only players'.[60] The aim of theatre is to satisfy neither its own practitioners nor scholars, except when either sit or stand in the auditorium, spectators among other spectators.

∼

I may seem to have wandered far from the quest for authenticity in 'Shakespearean' staging or performance. I have certainly expressed some scepticism about such quests, at least until they show the value of their finds in the shape of satisfied audiences. Every aspect of early texts that has been offered as evidence of what happened in the theatre, or of how the plays were acted, has turned out to be incapable of bearing the weight of interpretation laid on it. If excised passages are theatrical cuts, they relate to particular and irrecoverable circumstances of performance. If stage directions are long and graphic, they are more likely (like those of John Dover Wilson in his New Shakespeare editions in the 1920s) to be aimed at readers than to give an accurate account of what took place on stage. The punctuation of the quartos and First Folio, a straw still eagerly grasped at by some actors, may on occasion suggest a possible reading of a line, but it is authorial only in the surviving handful of autograph manuscripts; elsewhere it is the punctuation of scribes and compositors.

The Globe is not named on the title-page of any play quarto published before 1608,[61] the date of the King's Men's repossession of the Blackfriars, when it began to be necessary to remind purchasers which of the King's Men's two houses had been the site of performances of the play they were about to buy. Nor is it mentioned in the First Folio. When Heminges and Condell commend the plays to critical-minded readers, they do so in these terms:

> Censure will not driue a Trade, or make the Iacke go. And though you be a Magistrate of wit, and sit on the Stage at *Black-Friers*, or the *Cock-pit*, to arraigne Playes dailie, know, these Playes haue had their triall already, and stood out all Appeales; and do now come forth quitted rather by a Decree of Court, then any purchas'd Letters of commendation.[62]

By 1623 it was the audiences of the indoor playhouses who invited their attention (though no doubt those audiences also included many of the likeliest purchasers of so expensive a book). The Blackfriars, of course, was used in Shakespeare's lifetime, and speculation will continue about how far its facilities or its smaller size may have affected the stagecraft and verbal style of his latest plays. In 1623 the Cockpit, also known as the Phoenix, stood somewhere near the southern end of modern Drury Lane (its middle before the demolition of the southern end for the building of Bush House), outside the western limits of the City and in close proximity to the fashionable Strand. It was built at the end of 1616, some months after Shakespeare's death.

In the late 1960s Don Rowan drew attention to two drawings in the library of Worcester College, Oxford. They are in a collection of drawings by Inigo Jones, King's Surveyor and the most celebrated English architect of his time, and his assistant, John Webb. The four drawings, probably in the hand of Jones himself, are on two pages, and show a small playhouse, in plan, and in three elevations, of one end of the exterior and of the two ends of the interior, looking respectively towards the stage and the auditorium. The auditorium end is rounded like the apse of a church, the stage end rectangular. In 1969 Rowan was unable to relate the drawings to other evidence of playhouses built between 1605 and 1630 (the likely outer date limits for the drawings). He concluded: 'on balance I believe that one must proceed on the assumption that this Jones/ Webb theatre project was never realized, that it remains simply one further provocative design from the teeming mind of Inigo Jones.'[63] Later investigation by John Orrell opened up the interesting possibility that the plans might be for the conversion of a round building, the cock-fighting pit in Drury Lane, into a small playhouse – presumably the Cockpit or Phoenix itself.[64]

Whether or not Jones's design was ever realized in the seventeenth century, and whether or not it relates to the Cockpit, where Shakespeare's former colleague Christopher Beeston led Queen Anne's Men, it has been realized now, beside the new Globe. It will open in the near future as the 'Inigo Jones Theatre' – a name more exact than 'Shakespeare's

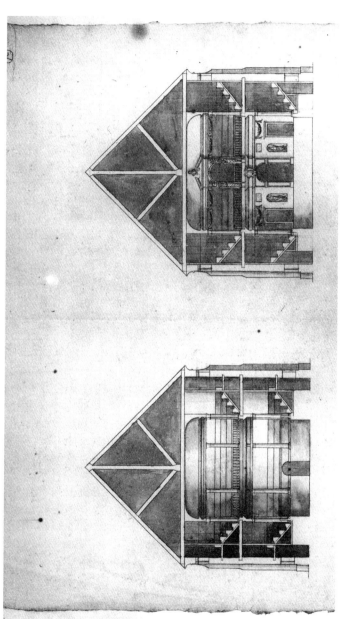

Figure 6 A design by Inigo Jones for a small playhouse, perhaps the Cockpit in Drury Lane (1616–17)

Globe' can possibly be. Why not, equally Burbage's Globe, or Fletcher's, Massinger's or James Shirley's Globe, to name only Shakespeare's successors in the direct line of 'ordinary poets' for the King's Men? The answer is self-evident: '*Shakespeare's*' Globe was the one that burnt down in 1613; theirs was its successor.

Was 'the Globe, the glory of Bankside', Shakespeare's ideal theatre, or may it rather have been a necessary makeshift, the only expedient open to the Burbages' company in the crisis of 1597–9 – in the course of which James Burbage died, leaving his sons Richard and Cuthbert to carry on the business – when Peter Allen repossessed the Theatre and the residents of Blackfriars successfully petitioned against the use of the indoor playhouse James had so providently been preparing since 1596? We cannot know, but Andrew Gurr's downbeat narrative of the events in *The Shakespearean Playing Companies* (1996) is persuasive in at least one detail.[65] Thatch was cheaper than roof-tiles, and the economy represented by thatching the First Globe was to prove a fatally false one when, on 29 June 1613, that same thatch caught fire during an early performance of *All Is True*, also known as *King Henry VIII*, and burnt their playhouse down.[66] The new Globe, as we learn from *Shakespeare's Globe Rebuilt*, should not repeat history in this particular. Its thatch 'has been laid on fire boards' and 'treated with a chemical fire retardant', and 'a drencher system has been incorporated in the roof'.[67]

The opening of the Inigo Jones Theatre will repeat history. The Globe company will acquire a winter-playing house, and the large repertoire of plays for the indoor playhouses, including perhaps Shakespeare's own *Cymbeline* and *The Tempest*, will be opened up to it. May it enjoy all the success of its famous predecessor, 'Shakespeare's Blackfriars'.

3

CANON

On a visit to Los Angeles a few years ago, I explained to the immigration officer at the International Airport that the purpose of my visit was to teach Shakespeare at UCLA. 'Shakespeare, huh? I read Shakespeare: every time he writes something new, I read it!' For a tired moment I toyed with the idea of an impromptu mini-lecture on two recent attributions, the short and inconsequential lyric 'Shall I die? Shall I fly ...?' and the ponderous and marble *Funeral Elegy in memory of the late virtuous Master William Peter of Whipton near Exeter,* 'by W. S', published in London in 1612. I then reflected that my chances of unimpeded entry to the US might be jeopardized, smiled politely, and passed through.

'Who wrote Shakespeare?' 'What did Shakespeare write?' In the words of two recent investigators (not members of a University English Department), 'These questions are seldom asked in English Departments these days. They are treated with the same kind of bristly nervousness that science departments show toward the UFO Question. Outside·English Departments, however, they remain an obsession'.[1]

~

During my teaching career in the English Department at King's College London I have experienced various manifestations of a Shakespeare 'canon'. When I arrived at King's in the 1960s, the University of London's English BA honours paper on Shakespeare required study of five 'set plays' (or four, if

Hamlet, which counted as two on account of its length, was among them). Some plays were never set, among them the three parts of *Henry VI, Titus Andronicus, The Two Gentlemen of Verona, Timon of Athens* and – unless memory deceives me – *Romeo and Juliet.* Uncertainty of authorship was among the grounds for exclusion, as well as the assumption – no doubt associated with that uncertainty – that some of 'Shakespeare's' plays just weren't good enough to be studied (or, in the case of *Romeo,* too popular for their own good). The number of 'set plays' subsequently shrank to three, and then compulsory 'Shakespeare' was accommodated not only by the traditional single-author paper but also by a new one on 'Shakespeare and Renaissance Literature'. Since then the study of Shakespeare has moved increasingly towards integration with other writers of his time and towards study of his plays as 'texts for performance'.

Performance has been for me the most valuable of all exercises in my own study of Shakespeare, as spectator, director and actor. I have had the great good fortune to direct six of his plays (if *Pericles* counts), four of them in the New Theatre of King's College, and to act in three of them. Indeed, the last words I spoke in that theatre, in 1984, were Gower's epilogue to *Pericles*:

> So, on your patience evermore attending,
> New joy wait on you! Here our play has ending.

Pericles, an apocryphal play, may serve as epigraph to my third lecture, on the occasion of my retirement.

∽

'Canon', transferred from its original reference to 'the books of the Bible accepted by the Christian Church as genuine and inspired', is defined by the *Oxford English Dictionary* as 'those writings of a secular author accepted as genuine'. 'Apocrypha' likewise originated in a biblical context, as 'those books included in the Septuagint and Vulgate versions of the Old Testament, which were not originally written in Hebrew and not counted genuine by the Jews, and which, at the Reformation, were excluded from the Sacred Canon by the Protestant party, as having no well-grounded claim to inspired authorship'. A *de facto* 'Shakespeare canon' was established by the First Folio in 1623 (though the Dictionary first records the use of the word in an edition of Shakespeare as late as 1953, in C.J. Sisson's single-volume edition – which includes the whole of an unfamiliar play, *Sir Thomas More*). *Pericles, Prince of Tyre* was not in the First Folio, though it had been in print as Shakespeare's since 1609. It did, however, head the first ever list of seven 'Shakespeare Apocrypha' in the 1664 Supplement to the Third Folio. Since the 1790s it has appeared in 'complete Shakespeares', and Shakespeare's authorship of *Pericles*, whether or not 'inspired', is accepted today as 'genuine', although he may have had a collaborator and there seems to be something wrong with the text, especially in the opening acts. The notion of a 'Shakespeare canon', that is to say, is less rigid and less sharply defined than is the case with the Old Testament.

Most of us own books that describe themselves as the *Works* or the *Complete Works* of William Shakespeare, but no publisher of such a collection has (to my knowledge) yet been successfully deterred by, or prosecuted under, the Trade Descriptions Act. Since the first attempt was made to publish a collection of Shakespeare's plays, the exact contents of *Shakespeare's Works* have fluctuated, but readers have been confident of finding among them the plays first published in 1623 as 'Mr. William Shakespeare's *Comedies, Histories, and Tragedies*', as well as – since the late eighteenth century – *Pericles* and non-dramatic writings including *Venus and Adonis, Lucrece* and the *Sonnets*. I shall not pursue the topic of the non-dramatic works, despite the presence of 'Shall I die?' in the Oxford Shakespeare (1986) and of the *Funeral Elegy* in the revised second edition of the *Riverside* Shakespeare (1997).[2]

At the end of the twentieth century, two terms I have used were under threat. 'Authorship' had been challenged as a non-entity, and seen as doubly problematic in relation to the frequently collaborative practices of Elizabethan and Jacobean script-writing.[3] Meanwhile, 'canons' were abhorred as restrictive practices by critics and theorists who wanted to impose other kinds of restriction, of their own choosing, on the study of literature.[4] 'Apocrypha', used by C.F. Tucker Brooke in the title of his 1908 edition of fourteen plays at some time attributed to Shakespeare,[5] is a term that loses its meaning if the significance of authorship and the concept of canonicity are denied. Brooke was sceptical about Shakespeare's share in any of his fourteen 'apocryphal' plays. For him, 'apocryphal' was equivalent to 'attributed to', if not merely – in another sense of the word – 'spurious'. Plays of unknown authorship have, of course, regularly been attributed to every known playwright of his period, but Shakespeare alone has been credited with 'Apocrypha'. Brooke's use of the term belonged to the imperial, Edwardian phase of bardolatry: it was a suitable fence to defend the inner sanctum from *un*inspired intruders. Even as late as 1974 Harry Levin could write, in his General Introduction to *The Riverside Shakespeare*, that 'Shakespeare's works have ... been accorded a place in our culture above and beyond their topmost place in our literature. They have been virtually canonized as humanistic scriptures, the texted residue of pragmatic wisdom, a general collection of quotable texts and usable examples.'[6] Of Brooke's fourteen plays, two now appear in editions of Shakespeare, three are believed to be by other known writers of the period, and many of the rest have been published in separate good editions.[7] These plays no longer need to be collected and labelled as 'Shakespeare Apocrypha'.

∽

The first book which claimed to include all Shakespeare's plays was, as I have said, the First Folio of 1623. The attempt of

Thomas Pavier, in 1619, to publish a ten-play collection of 'Shakespeare',[8] and the earlier quarto publication of half of Shakespeare's plays, 'stolne and surreptitious' or otherwise, apparently persuaded their owners, the King's Men, that it was better to accept what gains might follow from an authorized publication than to take the risk, after the thwarting of Pavier, of successful pre-emptive publication by someone else.

We do not know who established the contents of the First Folio – whether or not the 'care, and paine, to haue collected & publish'd them' were those of 'Iohn Heminges & Henry Condell' themselves. But their names – prominently displayed at the end of the dedication to the Herbert brothers, William, Earl of Pembroke, and Philip, Earl of Montgomery, and of the prefatory epistle to the '*great Variety of Readers*' – are the best testimony to the truth of the claim that this book contained, not only the most authentic text of the plays printed in it, but all the plays – not only those previously published but 'all the rest, absolute in their numbers, as he conceiued the*m*'. As the epistle points out, Shakespeare was 'by death departed from' the 'right' to oversee publication himself – a phrase which could imply that, had he survived, he might have given time and attention to such matters.[9] Before his death Shakespeare must have known of Ben Jonson's forthcoming Folio collection of his '*Works*', but we do not know whether the knowledge inspired in him any wish to see his own plays collected in a comparable volume.[10]

The signatories of the 'Epistle Dedicatorie' make altruistic gestures: the book is offered by them to its noble dedicatees '*vvithout ambition either of selfe-profit, or fame: onely to keepe the memory of so worthy a Friend, & Fellow aliue, as was our* SHAKESPEARE'.[11] The dedicatees are invited to act as guardians of Shakespeare's orphans (a role that implies equal concern for all his fatherless offspring). But the commercial motive for claiming completeness is also obvious. Piety and commercial profit have continued to motivate publishers and editors of

Shakespeare down the centuries. Heminges and Condell had the best qualifications for establishing a canon of Shakespeare's plays. They had worked with him in the Chamberlain's/King's company of players, Heminges since its inception in 1594, Condell since 1598: they appear in the Folio's list of 'the Principall Actors in all these Playes', Heminges third (after Shakespeare himself and Richard Burbage, who died in 1619, before the First Folio was planned), Condell eighth.[12] In addition, Heminges, as business manager of the company – jointly from 1596, then on his own from 1601 – was likelier than anyone else to know what payment had been made to whom for which playscript.[13]

They may have known less of Shakespeare's activities before 1594, during a period of nine years when he must have written some of the plays they included in the Folio and might, for all they knew, have written (or collaborated in writing) more. They would not have known of any moonlighting Shakespeare might have engaged in for other companies – if ever he found time (I here assume that he was bound by contract to write exclusively for his own company). Did Shakespeare write for any other company? We might guess not; yet even scholars who agree to identify 'Hand D' in *The Book of Sir Thomas More* as Shakespeare's are still divided on the question of when he put pen to that particular piece of paper. Much as one might prefer the tidier answer of 1593–4 (comfortably before the formation of the Chamberlain's Men[14]), the later date of 1601–2 remains a possibility. Either way, *Sir Thomas More* was not a Chamberlain's/King's play – and it isn't in the First Folio.

Of course Heminges and Condell knew that the Jaggards had not printed Shakespeare's *Complete Works*. To begin with, the Folio did not aim to reprint his non-dramatic poetry. And, when they claimed to have reprinted (with advantages) all the plays previously published as his and to have added 'all the rest', they must have been fully aware that the Folio had omitted *Troilus and Cressida*. It went on sale before *Troilus* was added to a second issue, stuck in between the Histories and the Tragedies, after hasty, last-minute printing. The preliminary pages of the Folio include not only the epistle in which Heminges and Condell promise readers *all* Shakespeare's plays, but a table of contents from which *Troilus* is missing. The epistle says nothing of this. When *Troilus* had initially to be removed from the place originally assigned to it among the Tragedies, probably for copyright reasons, the gap it left was filled by *Timon of Athens*. Would *Timon* have been printed in the Folio if no such gap had needed filling? And if *Timon* had not been included in the Folio would the epistle have alerted 'the great variety of readers' to the fact?[15]

If G.E. Bentley's evidence from documents relating to writers and companies active after 1616[16] can be read backwards into the lifetime of Shakespeare, then Shakespeare's own job description would have included the tasks of supplying (as occasion demanded) prologues, epilogues or additional dialogue for revivals of plays in the company's repertoire. Such additions were made, for instance, between 1606 and 1610, for a revival at court of the highly popular comedy of *Mucedorus*.[17] If Shakespeare did indeed supply the company with any additions and revisions, Heminges and Condell would hardly have thought that they should be printed in the Folio in the interests of completeness.

Collaboration is a further issue. Did Heminges and Condell admit to the Folio any play of which they knew Shakespeare was not the sole author? (Did their concern about his orphans extend to 'some bastards too'?) Collaborative playwriting was the norm rather than the exception in the public playhouses of Shakespeare's lifetime. The implication, that it was a practice he could and would have engaged in without qualms, was hard to accept in a climate of post-romantic idealization of Shakespeare as the 'national poet' or 'the Bard'. Scholarly investigation has found evidence of collaboration in some plays in the Folio, among them *Henry VIII*, in which most critics have little difficulty in discerning the hand of John Fletcher as well as that of Shakespeare.[18] No word is said of collaboration in the prefatory epistle.

The search for other playwrights in the Folio, starting with Edmond Malone's disintegration of the *Henry VI* plays in the 1780s,[19] reached its climax in the early years of the last century with that wholesale reassignment of plays and parts of plays which prompted E.K. Chambers's counter-attack in his 1924 lecture for the British Academy on 'The Disintegration of Shakespeare'.[20] Recently the focus has sharpened and narrowed onto those Folio plays, dating from about 1604–7, in which linguistic investigators have found characteristics they associate with Thomas Middleton, namely *Measure for Measure*, *Macbeth* and *Timon of Athens*.[21] John Fletcher's collaborative role in Shakespeare's latest plays, *Henry VIII* and *The Two Noble Kinsmen*, continues to attract attention, and a new open season has recently been declared on *1 Henry VI*,[22] while George Peele's authorship of the first act of *Titus Andronicus* still has champions.[23]

The Folio canon seems to have gone unchallenged in the years immediately following its publication, though it may be significant that the publication of the Second Folio in 1632 was followed in 1634 by a quarto edition of *The Two Noble Kinsmen*, 'Written by the memorable Worthies of their time; Mr. *Iohn Fletcher*, and Mr. *William Shakespeare*, Gent.', and in 1635 by the fifth quarto of the ever-popular *Pericles*, 'By William Shakespeare'. These quartos were printed respectively by the heirs to the Jaggards, the brothers and partners, Richard and Thomas Cotes. Buyers of Shakespeare's *Complete Works* since the 1970s may expect to find among them these two plays in which Shakespeare dramatized, with the aid of collaborators, two great fourteenth-century romances, 'The Knight's Tale' from Chaucer's *Canterbury Tales* and the story of Apollonius of Tyre from the eighth book of John Gower's *Confessio Amantis*.

Underlying the particular question of the canon of Shakespeare's plays is a theoretical issue with which I do not propose to engage, despite its final bearing on that question – the status and nature, if not the being or not-being, of 'the author'. My reasons for this evasion are: a secure confidence in the ample documentary evidence that playwrights regarded themselves, and were regarded by others, as authors in the period – after all, not only Heminges and Condell but also Ben Jonson, in his commendatory verses in the First Folio, refer to Shakespeare as 'the Author';[24] and a pragmatic conviction that belief in 'the death of the author' can safely be assumed to be premature until such time as publishers stop writing contracts and writers stop cashing their royalty cheques.

~

The picture that emerges so far is of a 'Shakespeare canon' that has a certain practical utility and is defined by the claims made in 1623 (though it remains a bit fuzzy round the edges). Two other collections of English plays were published in folio in the first half of the seventeenth century: Ben Jonson's in 1616 and 'Beaumont and Fletcher's' in 1647. Jonson's collection defines a self-made canon, although he does not draw attention to his exclusions, among them collaborative plays – *Eastward Ho* and the various plays for which *Henslowe's Diary* records payments to him – and his early comedy, *The Case is Altered*, which resurfaced only in the second half of the eighteenth century.[25] By contrast 'Beaumont and Fletcher' is a flag of convenience, useful to create a corpus of fashionable plays (fifty-one in the Second Folio of 1679) in genres, such as romantic tragicomedy, identifiable with John Fletcher, and in most of which Fletcher would indeed seem to have had a hand – though Beaumont is present in at most a dozen plays, many fewer than Fletcher's other principal collaborator and eventual successor, Philip Massinger.[26]

The concept of an authorial 'canon' involves the question of authentication (and the associated notion of property). In terms of authentication, the Jonson folio provides the best kind of testimony and the Shakespeare folio the second best, with 'Beaumont and Fletcher' doing little more than defining an area of investigation. In terms of property, publishers who will cut throats in pursuit of 'Shakespeare' and who, in the eighteenth century, made the issue of their perpetual right to publish him a test case in their fight against the establishment of authorial copyright, have as yet shown less energy in claiming Jonson or Fletcher. (In 1970 I published an edition of *The Two Noble Kinsmen.*[27] Following the precedent of the first edition of the play in 1634, I gave the names of its authors as John Fletcher and William Shakespeare, in that order. I have a suspicion that it might have earned more royalties over the years if I had been less scrupulous and put the big name first.) Although my topic is an authorial canon, I also wish to question the reluctance of publishers and readers to contemplate other criteria than the sometimes slippery one of authorship for constructing collections of plays, criteria which might reflect other, equally significant, common characteristics of the plays. Such collections might include the plays associated with particular acting companies, or with particular playhouses, or with particular moments in theatrical history; they would also allow for proper attention to plays of doubtful or unknown authorship. Some plays would be disqualified from inclusion in these collections too, but they would have the merit of restoring the plays of the best-known dramatists to the contexts of their original production and of allowing for the coherent study of related texts shaped for and by the same performers and playing conditions.

∼

I now turn to a different aspect of the 'Shakespeare canon': attribution to Shakespeare of plays not authorized by inclusion in the 1623 Folio. I shall make at least passing reference to a number of plays, printed between 1595 and 1728, or extant in manuscripts from Shakespeare's lifetime, which have claimed serious consideration in relation to his name. They are drawn from a much longer list. Writing in 1977, Lindley Williams Hubbell offered as 'a sufficient monument to human folly' a list of no fewer than seventy-five plays at some time attributed to Shakespeare which would constitute an 'Apocrypha' twice the size of the canon.[28]

It is surprising, given recent scholarly emphasis on the late construction of Shakespeare's reputation as supreme dramatist and national poet, how soon the attributions started. By the end of the seventeenth century, at least thirteen plays not in the First Folio had been attributed to Shakespeare, six of them in his lifetime. These six were printed in quartos that named 'W.S.', 'W. Shakespeare' or 'William Shakespeare' as their author or corrector. We can't be sure that 'W.S.' pointed at Shakespeare, but three of these plays, *The True Chronicle History of the Whole Life and Death of Thomas Lord Cromwell* (1602) 'Written by W.S.', *The London Prodigal* (1605) 'By VVilliam Shakespeare*' and *A Yorkshire Tragedy* (1608) 'VVritten by VV. Shakspeare', belonged to his company. Before 1700 the plays most readily attributed to him were romantic comedies and English histories, with a topical and moralizing murder play, *A Yorkshire Tragedy*, thrown in for full measure.[29] Attributions from the 1650s to the 1670s were mainly, and casually, made in entries of play manuscripts on the Stationers' Register or in booksellers' play-lists, bound in printed plays to advertise their stock. After the Restoration one more play was printed as Shakespeare's. This was *The Birth of Merlin*, published by Francis Kirkman and Henry Marsh in 1662 with attribution to Shakespeare and William Rowley. One of the more casual attributions, *The Reign of King Edward III*, blithely lumped together in a bookseller's list with Marlowe's *Edward II* and Thomas Heywood's *Edward IV* as Shakespeare's,[30] was to be repeated on more reasoned grounds in the eighteenth century and since.

More substantial than these attributions by association are records that link the name of Shakespeare with that of his younger colleague John Fletcher, who was to succeed him as principal dramatist for the King's Men. I have already mentioned *The Two Noble Kinsmen* and its adoption in recent years into the Shakespeare canon. Two intriguing and enigmatic references, dating from 1613, have been found to a lost play of '*Cardenno*' or '*Cardenna*'. On 20 May and 9 July 1613 the King's Men's business manager, John Heminges, was paid for two performances of it at court.[31] It seems likely that this was the same play that was entered on the Stationers' Register by Humphrey Moseley on 9 September 1653 as 'The History of Cardenio, by M[r]. Fletcher, & Shakespeare'.[32] So far as we know, Moseley never published it. It too was to resurface, in 1727, though under a different name and without reference to the documentary record.[33]

To return to the late seventeenth century: the 'apocryphal' status of plays printed with attributions to Shakespeare or 'W.S.' was established in 1664, when Philip Chetwynd collected seven of them to supplement a reissue of the Third Folio.[34] His principles of selection were evidently either that an earlier printed edition of the play attributed it to Shakespeare or could be alleged to have suggested such an attribution, and that the edition making the claim dated (or purported to date) from Shakespeare's lifetime. The seven plays were reprinted in the Fourth Folio in 1685, and continued to appear with some frequency in eighteenth-century editions of Shakespeare. Thus in 1780 they appeared, under the editorial care of Edmond Malone, in the second volume of a *Supplement* to the edition of Shakespeare's plays by Samuel Johnson and George Steevens published in 1778. They were annotated with the opinion of Malone, as well as those of Steevens and earlier scholars, as to their right to be there. Only *Pericles* was to survive within the Shakespeare canon.

Here is Steevens on *The Tragedy of Locrine*, a neo-Senecan tragedy of mythic British kings, first printed in 1595 with the claim that it had been 'Newly set foorth, ouerseene and corrected, By *VV. S.*': 'the piece itself affords abundant internal evidence that not a single line of it was written by Shakspeare.... I think we may safely pronounce it to be the work of some academick, whose learning was ostentatious, and whose merriment was low.'[35]

Not to be outdone, Malone weighed in:

> The scene of the greater part of this play being laid in a wood, through which the editor confesses himself too dim-sighted to discern his way, it has been found impracticable to give any clear description of the different places where the various personages of this drama recite their tedious and uninteresting declamations; and therefore nothing of that kind has been attempted.[36]

The dismissal of these six plays, however unfairly conducted, has not been followed by any sustained appeal. By common consent, even the three that are not now believed to be the work of other writers offer nothing that can easily be read as evidence that Shakespeare wrote them. The 1664 *Supplement* to the Third Folio represents an attempt to tidy the Shakespeare canon by impounding strays, rather than by originating any serious inquiry into their authorship. In the decade that saw the first radical adaptations of Shakespeare for changed theatrical conditions, it may seem more remarkable that the effort was made at all than that it lacked critical rigour or discrimination.

~

New attributions since the eighteenth century present quite a different picture. From Lewis Theobald's *Double Falsehood* in 1727, each new attribution involved its backer in mounting the increasingly radical (and decreasingly plausible) claim

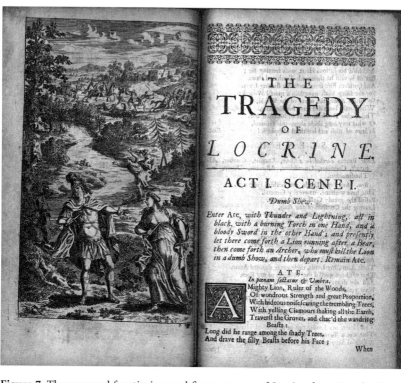

THE
TRAGEDY
OF
LOCRINE.

ACT I. SCENE I.

Dumb Shew.

Enter Ate, with Thunder and Lightning, all in black, with a burning Torch in one Hand, and a bloody Sword in the other Hand; and presently let there come forth a Lion running after a Bear; then come forth an Archer, who must kill the Lion in a dumb Show, and then depart. Remain Ate.

ATE.

In pœnam sectatur & Umbra.

Mighty Lion, Ruler of the Woods,
Of wondrous Strength and great Proportion,
With hideous noise scaring the trembling Trees,
With yelling Clamours shaking all the Earth,
Travers't the Groves, and chac'd the wandring
  Beasts :
Long did he range among the shady Trees,
And drave the silly Beasts before his Face ;

When

Figure 7 The engraved frontispiece and first text page of *Locrine*, from Rowe's edition of Shakespeare, vol. 6 (1709)

that he had hooked that elusive fish – an unknown, or at least unrecognized, play by Shakespeare. These claims were not based, like the earliest attributions, on any external documentary reference to Shakespeare, or even 'W.S.', as author or part-author, but were argued on circumstantial grounds, or on the strength of a range of purportedly evidential features of the play itself. With the exhaustion of known 'external evidence', the era of 'internal evidence' had begun.

By 1727 the commercial value of the name of Shakespeare had already risen and the Copyright Act of 1710 had finally codified the right of authors to profit from their labours, for a period of fourteen or twenty-eight years. Theobald, recently in the eye of the literary world after publication of *Shakespeare Restored* (1726), his savage book-length review of Alexander Pope's edition of Shakespeare, took full advantage of both considerations. The play he presented, first in December 1727 on the boards of the Drury Lane Theatre, then in print in 1728, was described on its title-page as Theobald's own adaptation of one 'Written Originally by *W. SHAKESPEARE*'. The royal privilege for sole copyright in the play for fourteen years, granted directly by George II to 'our Trusty, and Well-beloved *Lewis Theobald*, of our City of *London*, Gent.', was prominently printed, facing the title-page. Theobald rightly anticipated an incredulous reception: unfortunately, in the first version of his 'Preface' to the play, he overstated his case for Shakespeare's authorship of the original. In a reissue, designated the second edition, he altered and extended the offending passage. In its first version, it read:

> Others again, to depreciate the Affair, as they thought, have been pleased to urge, that tho' the Play may have some Resemblances of *Shakespeare*, yet the *Colouring*, *Diction*, and *Characters*, come nearer to the Style and Manner of FLETCHER. This, I think, is far from deserving any Answer; I submit it to the Determination of better Judgments; tho' my Partiality for *Shakespeare* makes me wish, that Every Thing which is good, or pleasing, in our Tongue, had been owing to his Pen.[37]

For the 'second edition' Theobald changed and amplified the final sentence.

> tho' my Partiality for *Shakespeare* makes me wish, that Every Thing which is good, or pleasing, in that other great Poet [i.e. Fletcher], had been owing to *his* Pen. I had once design'd a *Dissertation* to prove this Play to be of *Shakespeare*'s Writing, from some of its remarkable Peculiarities in the *Language*, and Nature of the *Thoughts*: but as I could not be sure but that the Play might be attack'd, I found it adviseable, upon second Consideration, to reserve *that* Part of my *Defence....* I therefore think it not amiss here to promise, that, tho' *private Property* should so far stand in my Way, as to prevent me from putting out an *Edition* of *Shakespeare*, yet some Way or other, if I live, the Publick shall receive from my Hand his *whole* WORKS corrected, with my best Care and Ability. This may furnish an Occasion for speaking more at large concerning the present Play: For which Reason I shall now drop it for another Subject.[38]

Having dropped the subject, Theobald never picked it up again, nor is he known ever to have shown anyone the three manuscripts that he claimed to have purchased at considerable expense. *Double Falsehood* is absent alike from his edition of Shakespeare and from the edition of Beaumont and Fletcher that he initiated in the 1730s. Two views of this affair are current: Theobald was a liar and his play merely a forgery; Theobald was right in supposing that he had copies of a Jacobean play, but made the error of supposing what was really a Shakespeare/Fletcher collaboration to be exclusively the work of the former. He offered no documentary evidence for the attribution to Shakespeare.

Double Falsehood has been seen, however, as a radical adaptation of the 'lost' *Cardenio*, acted by the King's Men in 1613, to the changed theatrical conditions of the early eighteenth century. Its plot derives from the episodic narrative of the tribulations of Cardenio, Luscinda and Dorotea and the villainy of Don Fernando found in the third and fourth books of Cervantes's *Don Quixote*.[39] Theobald knew of this source and pointed out that its London publication in the English

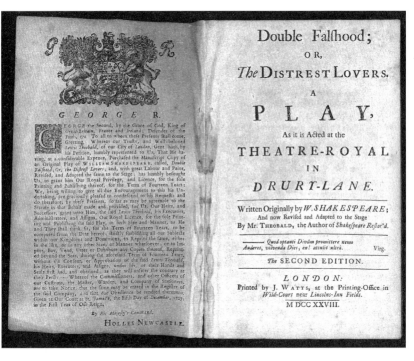

Figure 8 Opening of Lewis Theobald's edition of *Double Falsehood* (1728, second issue), showing the royal patent granting him copyright in the play

version by Thomas Shelton had taken place in 1611 (more exactly, at the beginning of 1612). Shelton made his translation some five years earlier, probably from the Spanish text published at Brussels in 1607. Theobald claimed that among the three manuscripts of the play he had purchased one was 'of above Sixty Years Standing, in the Hand-writing of Mr. Downes, the famous Old Prompter; and, ... was early in the possession of the celebrated Mr. *Betterton*, and by Him design'd to have been usher'd into the World'. Of his other two manuscripts, one was less old, but 'One of them is much more perfect, and has fewer Flaws and Interruptions in the Sense.'[40]

Recent scholarship inclines towards vindicating Theobald.[41] Vestigial but recognizable traces of linguistic and metrical characteristics of both Shakespeare and Fletcher have been detected, and, even if he knew of them, Theobald certainly made no reference to the Jacobean records or to Moseley's Stationers' Register entry of *Cardenio* in 1653. The optimistic version of the story is that Theobald had purchased the very manuscript entered by Humphrey Moseley in 1653 (the 'more perfect' manuscript) and one or more drafts of an adaptation that Betterton had commissioned in the early 1660s but had never staged. In 1666 Sir William Davenant adapted *The Two Noble Kinsmen* as *The Rivals*, a version which jettisoned almost all the bits we think of as Shakespeare's but retained much from the stylistically simpler Fletcher scenes.[42] Had a similar fate befallen *Cardenio*, the sparseness of the traces of Shakespeare in *Double Falsehood* would at once be explicable, especially as it would then be twice a palimpsest – Theobald's own reworking of a previous reworking of the Jacobean original for Betterton sixty years earlier. One or other adapter changed the names of the leading characters to Julio, Leonora, Violante (archetypal victim of seduction and desertion) and Henriquez, but the outline of the attenuated action is recognizably that of Cervantes's narrative, and much verbal detail corresponds more closely with Shelton's version of it than with any other English version before 1727.[43] Had Theobald forged the play, it is hard to see why its language should show (as it does) clearer vestiges of the style and metre of Fletcher (whose participation he denied) than of those of Shakespeare (to whom he wished to attribute it all).[44]

Theobald was much ridiculed and his later silence may have been motivated in part by embarrassment.[45] The royal licence seemed to authorize the attribution solely to Shakespeare, about which he must himself have come to harbour doubts – also he may have wanted to enjoy his profits (though they can't have been great, since the only reprint within his fourteen-year copyright was a Dublin piracy in 1728). The stage history of *Double Falsehood* extends to the 1790s, with one later revival in 1847. A newspaper reference in 1770 to a manuscript of the play as being 'treasured up in the Museum of Covent Garden Playhouse' is merely tantalizing, as the theatre and its library were destroyed by fire in 1808.[46]

In the heavily adapted state in which *Cardenio* survives as *Double Falsehood*, it is hard to discern its likely original structure. Scenically, it is of the 1720s; its action unfolds before visual representations of '*A Royal Palace*', '*The Prospect of a Village*' and '*A Wide Plain, with a Prospect of Mountains at a Distance*'. Its female roles, played at Drury Lane by Mrs Porter and Mrs Booth, contain some of the Jacobean verse fossils, but have presumably been written up for the tastes of the eighteenth-century audience. Among the fossils, this exchange between Leonora and her suitor Julio, who has just been ordered to court, seemed to Kenneth Muir representative of late Shakespearean phrasing and rhythm.[47]

JUL.
    Urge not suspicions of what cannot be;
    You deal unkindly, mis-becomingly,
    I'm loth to say: For All that waits on you,
    Is graced, and graces. – No Impediment

Shall bar my Wishes, but such grave Delays
As Reason presses Patience with; which blunt not,
But rather whet our Loves. Be patient, Sweet.

LEON.

Patient! What else? My Flames are in the Flint.
Haply, to lose a Husband I may weep;
Never, to get One: When I cry for Bondage,
Let Freedom quit me.[48]

The villainous Don Henriquez, who seduces and abandons
Violante before first attempting to marry the reluctant
Leonora and then, after her escape, pursuing her into a
nunnery by pretending to be a corpse in a coffin, is the star
role. Mr Wilks, who played it, also spoke the Prologue. For the
Epilogue, the services of the celebrated Mrs Oldfield were
called upon. The story – in *Don Quixote* a retrospective
narrative by the self-exiled and demented Cardenio (Julio in
the play) – is dramatized in chronological sequence, without
developing much more than narrative interest. It lacks the
comic byplay or interwoven subplot that one would expect in
a Jacobean romantic tragicomedy. In the manner of late
Shakespeare, the action moves from court to country, and its
happy denouement, in which Julio recovers his beloved Leonora
and the misdemeanours of Henriquez are conveniently
obliterated by marriage to his victim Violante, includes the
fathers of the two girls – once again after the 'family reunion'
pattern of late Shakespeare. Though Theobald would seem to
have had a Jacobean original before him, in adapting it he was
affected by his intimate knowledge of Shakespeare. The play
abounds in verbal echoes, chiefly of such less well-known plays
as *The Two Gentlemen of Verona, Troilus and Cressida, All's
Well that Ends Well* and *Cymbeline.* Despite the recent
ingenious attempt of Richard Wilson to relate it to the public
events of the winter of 1612–13 – an attempt that depends on
retaining Cervantes's name for 'Cardenio' (Robert Carr) and

adopting Theobald's name for 'Henriquez' (Prince Henry) – the play seems resolutely unpolitical.[49]

That *Double Falsehood* should enter the Shakespeare canon may seem an unlikely proposition – if we continue subconsciously to regard canonic status as a reflection of literary merit rather than of historical fact (as I fear I have myself done in my disparaging remarks on 'Shall I die?' and *A Funeral Elegy*). On the evidence, I have little doubt that in *Double Falsehood* we have a text that may be characterized as 'The Ghost of *Cardenio*'. Its interest lies in its relation to the other Shakespeare/Fletcher collaborations and it therefore belongs beside them in its own corner of the Shakespeare and Fletcher canons, or in the Jacobean repertoire of the King's Men. Only when it is duly placed there will the further study that may reveal more of its chequered history become possible. I have dwelt at some length on *Double Falsehood*, since it alone of the plays attributed to Shakespeare in the eighteenth and nineteenth centuries on grounds of any substance cannot yet be studied in an adequate and up-to-date edition.

I could, at this point, call the roll of further serious attributions through the last three centuries. Instead, I shall focus on two more plays which (like *Double Falsehood*) are prime candidates for inclusion in all complete Shakespeares. In fact both plays, *King Edward III* and *Sir Thomas More*, are more than just 'candidates': they have already attained some measure of canonical acceptance.

The earliest substantial claim for *The Reign of King Edward III* was made by the Cambridge scholar Edward Capell in a sample volume of edited texts, under the title of *Prolusions*, which he published in 1760, before undertaking his complete edition of Shakespeare. Capell staked his claim as follows:

> But what shall be said of the poem that constitutes the second part? or how shall the curiosity be satisfy'd, which it is probable may have been raised by the great Name inserted in the title-page? That it was indeed written by SHAKESPEARE, it cannot be said with candour that there is any external evidence at all: something of proof arises from resemblance between the stile of his earlier performances and of the work in question; and a more conclusive one yet from consideration of the time it appear'd in, in which there was no known writer equal to such a play: the fable of it too is taken from the same books which that author is known to have follow'd in some other plays; to wit, *Holinshed*'s Chronicle, and a book of novels call'd the Palace of Pleasure: But, after all, it must be confess'd that it's being his work is conjecture only, and matter of opinion; and the reader must form one of his own, guided by what is now before him, and by what he shall meet with in perusal of the piece itself.[50]

By the end of the last century Capell's proposal had won enough support (much of it in Germany) for *Edward III* to be included in at least one complete Shakespeare. F.J. Furnivall printed Nicolas Delius's text of it in 1877 in his 'Leopold' Shakespeare. It did not reappear in any complete Shakespeare until 1997, when the revised second edition of the *Riverside* Shakespeare took the bold step of adding it, if not quite to the canon, then at least to an appendix of attributed works. In 1998 the New Cambridge Shakespeare published an edition of it by the eminent Italian Shakespeare scholar, Giorgio Melchiori, which accepts the attribution of at least parts of it to Shakespeare.[51]

Unlike *Pericles, Cardenio* or *The Two Noble Kinsmen*, which belong to the latter end of Shakespeare's playwriting career, *Edward III*, first printed at the beginning of 1596, may well have been written some three or four years before that date, that is to say, before the formation of the Chamberlain's Men in 1594. No contemporary statement attaches it to Shakespeare, or to any other playwright or playwrights. It may be of collaborative authorship, but if so the identity of the other writer or writers remains to be established. It is the only play whose attribution to Shakespeare has been persuasively argued entirely on internal grounds of its congruence, in whole or in part, with what we know of the poetic, metrical, linguistic, thematic and dramatic qualities of Shakespeare's attested plays.

As has several times been remarked, if Shakespeare didn't write *Edward III*, then he should have done. It dramatizes the first part of the story of the Hundred Years War, relating the youthful exploits of the Black Prince in battle to his father King Edward's battles against the Scots, against the virtue of the Countess of Salisbury, wife of one of his generals, and against his own dishonourable lust. The so-called 'Countess episode', staged several times by William Poel as a one-act play under the title of 'The King and the Countess',[52] has always been the focus of attempts to urge Shakespeare's authorship. It anticipates the attempted seduction of Isabella by Angelo in *Measure for Measure* and it is pervaded by the language of the *Henry VI* plays and of the *Sonnets* (most famously in the shared line, 'Lilies that fester smell far worse than weeds'[53]).

∽

As time went by, printed plays to father on Shakespeare grew harder to find; but there were still the manuscripts. Of these, *The Book of Sir Thomas More* is likely to remain a subject of intense scrutiny. This play was first edited in 1844, for the recently established Shakespeare Society, by Alexander Dyce, from the manuscript, which by then was already 'Harleian 7368' in the library of the British Museum. According to Dyce's brief preface, it

> is written in several hands, a portion of it appearing to have belonged to a playhouse transcript: in some places it is slightly mutilated; and in others it presents so much confusion from the scenes having been re-modelled and the leaves misplaced, that considerable difficulty has been experienced in preparing a copy for the press.

> Concerning the author of this tragedy nothing is known. It would
> seem to have been composed towards the close of the sixteenth century
> (about 1590, or perhaps a little earlier); but there are some grounds for
> supposing that a few additions were made to it at a later period.[54]

In 1871 Richard Simpson claimed that about a third of the
manuscript was in a hand that he identified as that of
Shakespeare.[55] Forty years later, the claim was reduced to three
pages by W.W. Greg, whose edition of the manuscript for the
Malone Society remains a necessary point of reference.[56] Greg
differentiated six hands: 'Hand S', that of the copyist of the
original manuscript, whom he identified as the playwright
and pamphleteer Anthony Munday; 'Hand C', that of a
professional theatrical scribe whose annotations survive in
other theatrical manuscripts; and Hands A to E, those of four
writers of additional or revised sections of the text. The
revisers too were identified by Greg and others: 'Hand A' was
Henry Chettle; 'Hand B' possibly Thomas Heywood; 'Hand E'
Thomas Dekker. The longest revision, the three-page section
by 'Hand D' numbered by Greg as 'Addition IIc', was identified
as the work of Shakespeare, written in his own hand as he
composed it.[57]

Following Greg's edition, a collection of essays published
in 1923 as *Shakespeare's Hand in 'The Book of Sir Thomas
More'*[58] brought together various categories of evidence for
the identification, from the palaeographic to the political
(the scene in question is one in which More, as sheriff of
London, quells with his eloquence the famous 'Ill May Day'
riot of 1517, when Londoners rose in violent protest against
resident foreigners). Later study was to add a further short
soliloquy for More to Shakespeare's share, but this was
copied in Hand C.[59] The 'Hand D' scene took a central place
in all subsequent discussions of Shakespeare's texts, notably
in the work of Dover Wilson, whose contribution to the
collection was an essay on 'Hand D' and the spellings found

in the 'good' quartos (most of which are amply available elsewhere too).[60]

By 1989 the wheel had turned, if not quite come full circle. *Shakespeare and 'Sir Thomas More': Essays on the Play and its Shakespearian Interest*, edited by Trevor Howard-Hill, reflects the turn in the very coolness of its title, and the essays in it indicate that all questions are still open. In the view of the editor, however, 'The balance of arguments presented in the present volume, most readers will agree, tips the balance further in favour of Shakespeare as the author and hand of Addition IIc, and ... for the first time establishes a respectable case for the revision of *More* after 1600.'[61]

The late dating, of course, is problematic for the attribution to Shakespeare. 'Hand D', we are now told, didn't know the original text for which he supplied his revision (which might argue for early dating), but 'the stylistic evidence which links' the three pages 'with plays of his middle period tells against him as collaborator in the early text' and urges a late dating of 'Addition IIc'.[62] The two books about *Sir Thomas More* reflect two changes in the assumptions of Elizabethan dramatic scholarship: a new scepticism about questions of attribution and a shift of emphasis towards the view of surviving plays as 'texts for performance'. Where the 1923 collection of essays found its focus in the handwriting, the links with the 'good' quartos and 'the expression of ideas – particularly political ideas' in the Hand D addition, in 1989 the topics included 'dates and acting companies' and 'The date and auspices of the additions', while the playwrights discussed include Henry Chettle and John Webster (though the latter figures only in a refutation by Charles Forker of the suggestion that Webster, rather than Shakespeare, might be 'Hand D'[63]). *Sir Thomas More*, then, has held its place as a plausible recruit to the Shakespeare canon – in respect of the three pages.

What has yet to receive the attention it deserves is the authorship of the original play. As Munday copied it, it has been easily assumed that he was at least part-author of it. If David Bradley, in his study of George Peele and Lord Strange's Men,[64] is right, and the term 'plotter' refers to a particular function within the playhouses, the 'plotter' being the man whose job it is to fit a play text to the available cast and otherwise oversee its readiness for performance, then the role of Anthony Munday is due for reassessment. When Francis Meres conducted his 1598 survey of the English literary scene in *Palladis Tamia: Wit's Treasury*, Munday, together with many more writers for the stage, received mention – as 'our best plotter'.[65] The phrase has caused some perplexity. Did Munday run a 'rent-a-plot' agency for overworked playwrights? Was the reference after all to his own achievements as a dramatist? If, however, he was applauded as the best fitter-up of texts for performance – the best *Dramaturg* – then one large assumption about *Sir Thomas More* might be challenged (with implications for the other surviving manuscript play in his hand, an engaging comedy of rival magicians called *John a Kent and John a Cumber*[66]). It has been assumed that no playwright other than its author would be likely to transcribe a whole play. Now we may have to consider the possibility that Munday, who did write plays, may also have had a job that entailed copying them out, whether or not he was their author. He certainly had good qualifications for employment as a scribe. His hand was neat and small, and (on the surviving evidence) he could save paper by getting more legible lines on to a folio page than many of his contemporaries.

~

It is more than time to return from case histories to wider issues.

What, in a case of assignment of authorship, constitutes 'proof'?

We may start with the robust statement of George Kane, writing of the authorship of the great fourteenth-century poem *Piers Plowman*.

In a case of ascription the character of external evidence is that it exists absolutely, in some determinable way independent of the text which it concerns. It may be bad; its accuracy can be questioned, but its existence cannot. It is a kind of physical fact. Internal evidence, by contrast, is a critical postulate. It has a contingent character, depending for its existence on being identified as such by someone, and for its validity upon, first, the correctness of the identification, and second, the quality of the reasoning applied to it.[67]

The investigator's tasks are to evaluate the reliability of 'external' evidence, and to validate or reject 'internal' evidence in terms of its significance and relevance. In the case of several Shakespearean 'Apocrypha' both categories of evidence exist and must be balanced against each other.

I don't believe that *The London Prodigal* is, as its 1605 title-page claimed, 'By VVilliam Shakespeare', unless that claim can be construed as referring to his status as chief playwright of 'the Kings Maiesties seruants' and thus, by implication, in some way responsible for all its repertoire.[68] As 'external' evidence, this title-page contains a claim about the playing company that *can* be credited and an authorship attribution that can*not*. In reaching this conclusion I am letting negative 'internal evidence' (or the lack of positive) affect my estimate of the 'external' claim on the title-page.

The potential power of good external evidence is, however, revealed by a recent discovery. The office-book of Sir Henry Herbert, Master of the Revels from the 1620s into the Restoration, was re-edited by Nigel Bawcutt in 1996. The new edition incorporates entries collected from various sources, some previously unpublished. Among these is an entry dated 1622: 'The *Childe hath founde the Father*, for perusing and allowing of a New Play, Acted by the Princes Seruants at the Curtayne, 1622 1*li*.' Bawcutt's note identifies this as 'an alternative title for William Rowley's *The Birth of Merlin*, published 1662. This has previously been dated either 1608 or 1621–2; [Sir John Astley's] licence confirms the later date.'[69]

A single, reliable piece of external evidence has reduced by one the roster of Shakespeare Apocrypha. Kirkman's 1662 attribution of *The Birth of Merlin* to Rowley and Shakespeare is wrong; it dates, not, as hitherto seemed plausible, from the first or second decade of the seventeenth century, but from the third; it was played at the Curtain, and Prince Charles's Men played it. The attribution to Shakespeare never won much credence, but it did distract attention from other aspects of the play – at least until Joanna Udall published her edition in 1991.[70] One sad fact about the attributions I have listed is the extent to which focus on authorship attribution can blind investigators to all other aspects of the plays in question. Who acted a play, or where it was acted, are facts of comparable significance – and they are facts that can sometimes be ascertained by analysis of surviving texts (including analysis of minimum casting requirements).

In the cases of *Sir Thomas More*, *Edward III* and *Double Falsehood* 'external evidence' is non-existent, or at best circumstantial. Authorship of these plays can only be established, if at all, by analysis of whatever features of the texts may reveal the linguistic, or other, habits of writers whose habits are sufficiently distinctive for recognition and sufficiently stable over a large enough body of undisputed work. Shakespeare, Thomas Middleton, John Fletcher and Philip Massinger are such dramatists. Less confidence is attainable for others, Anthony Munday, Henry Chettle, George Peele and Robert Greene among them, because so little exists by way of reliable 'control texts'. Even Christopher Marlowe presents difficulties, as his six plays survive in disparate texts published at widely differing dates.

The search for 'internal evidence' of Shakespeare's authorship, as my illustrations have indicated, has been unsystematic. It began as a search for likenesses between the candidate for canonization and the attested 'works', in the form of 'parallel passages', or similar metrical characteristics, or shared ideas.

As the study of Elizabethan and Jacobean drama expanded in the nineteenth and twentieth centuries, standards of evidence for similarity became more rigorous when it became more and more apparent that writers of the period were brought up on a doctrine of literary 'imitation' which did not preclude borrowing or adapting material from other texts, and on a diet of proverbial wisdom and emblematic imagery which supplied a wide vocabulary of shared allusive commonplaces. The romantic notion of the organic, individual 'poet' yielded gradually to a clearer sense of the constraints under which writers worked to supply the commercial playhouses with a steady succession of new plays (many of them more or less skilful recyclings of other plays). Shakespeare took his material where he found it (including the repertoire of the Queen's Men, to which he may have belonged at some date before 1594[71]). The study of his 'sources' led to Geoffrey Bullough's monumental edition, in eight volumes published between 1957 and 1975, of those 'narrative and dramatic' works that can certainly or probably be identified as having been on his reading-list, or even his desk, as he wrote each play.[72]

The individuality of Shakespeare is apparent to actors and students, to spectators and readers, but it is not easily resolved into transferable formulas which can form the basis of statistical demonstration of what he did or did not write. In recent years, however, two new models of enquiry have promised fresh kinds of 'internal evidence' for authorship investigations. These are stylometric and socio-linguistic analysis of the language of Elizabethan and Jacobean plays. 'Stylometry' attempts to construct, on the basis of statistical computer analysis of large quantities of text, a 'linguistic fingerprint' for each of the writers under investigation. The 'fingerprints' can then be used to differentiate between writers, and thus to draw lines of demarcation between what each playwright wrote. The linguistic habits studied are selected from the stratum of usage that is likely to be beneath the level of conscious stylistic control (a fact that renders the label 'stylometry' less than wholly helpful[73]). The existence of such differences had long been familiar to earlier investigators. Cyrus Hoy's work on the Beaumont and Fletcher canon, or Peter Lake's on Middleton, recognized reflex linguistic habits distinctive of each writer involved, including habits of colloquial elision, 'Ile', 'y'are', ''em', 'let's' and the like.[74] Fletcher prefers 'ye' to 'you', and 'has' and 'does' to 'hath' and 'doth'. Stylometry goes further, computing the relative frequency with which two writers use common words, 'no' or 'not', say, or particular combinations of words that make up common phrases, or how often they use 'with' as the penultimate word in a sentence.

At the start of my lecture I quoted, anonymously, a comment on the obsessive public curiosity about Shakespearean authorship. Its authors were Professors Ward Elliott and Robert Valenza, of Claremont McKenna College in California. In the mid-1980s they set up a 'Shakespeare Clinic', which undertook to look at Shakespearean attributions as a test case in the statistical study of language. Neither they nor their college have a primary concern with the humanities. This gave them a less professionally engaged or interested stake in their results than most investigators, though they sought the advice of specialists in the field of Elizabethan drama at every stage of their project and engaged in dialogue (sometimes acrimonious on the part of their respondents) with other investigators.[75]

Where previous investigations had concentrated on finding a correspondence between 'Shakespeare' and putative rival authors or attributed texts (what the Clinicians call 'green-light' tests), they proposed the alternative of 'red-light' testing. A set of linguistic habits derived from the canonical texts was established as a 'Shakespearean' profile and this profile was then used to test the claims of the rival poets and texts in terms of their 'fit'. Ten rejections, and the rival was out!

Of course, the results as formally presented are less crude and more carefully qualified than my tabloid reduction suggests. Those results, published in *Computers and the Humanities* in 1996, were simple.

> The Shakespeare Clinic has developed 51 computer tests of Shakespeare play authorship and 14 of poem authorship, and applied them to 37 claimed 'true Shakespeares', to 27 plays of the Shakespeare Apocrypha, and to several poems of unknown or disputed authorship. No claimant, and none of the apocryphal plays or poems, matched Shakespeare. Two plays and one poem from the Shakespeare Canon, *Titus Andronicus*, *Henry VI*, Part 3, and 'A Lovers' Complaint', do not match the others.[76]

Their article bore the felicitous title 'And Then There Were None'. Though undogmatic about the significance of their results and open to rejection by better methodology, Elliott and Valenza reasonably concluded:

> It is hard now to believe either that [Shakespeare] could have been a committee, or that any claimant's poem or corpus, or any Apocrypha poem or play, or any play from the Dubitanda, now augmented by *3H6* and *Titus Andronicus*, could have been written by him *solo*.[77]

They did not claim equal confidence in their results for texts of collaborative authorship. Their criteria admitted the Jacobean *Henry VIII* and *Timon of Athens*, including the sections attributed to Fletcher and Middleton, but rejected overall Shakespearean authorship of two much disputed early plays. They conceded that this outcome might result from something not being 'quite right', either in the conventional authorship divisions or in their own tests. Another stylometrist, Thomas Merriam, is currently at work on a programme for discerning the points in a text where a change of linguistic characteristics may indicate a shift from one collaborating author to another.[78] Such studies will no doubt multiply with the easy availability of more and more electronic texts. Improving the sensitivity and flexibility will be a task for the future

strength of stylometric analysis lies in its speed and its power over large quantities of material (its development has depended on the ability of computers to handle those quantities); its weakness, in a much-voiced criticism, is that it doesn't always know what it is counting.

Socio-linguistics, exemplified by the work of Jonathan Hope in *The Authorship of Shakespeare's Plays*[79] takes a different line with linguistic variation between playwrights and seeks explanations for it rather than quantitative evidence of its presence. If Fletcher and Shakespeare differ, as they do in their preferences for 'you' or 'ye', 'hast' or 'has', 'ay' or 'yes', then there must be a reason. That reason is not far to seek. Shakespeare grew up in the Midlands in the 1560s and 1570s; Fletcher in London and Kent in the 1580s and 1590s. Shakespeare's father was a tradesman; Fletcher's a bishop. The period of the major drama of Elizabethan and Jacobean London was one of rapid linguistic change: the direction of change was towards a greater regularity, encouraged in principle by linguistic theorists and in practice by the growing dominance of metropolitan culture and the operations of the printing press. Writers of different ages and backgrounds had different linguistic habits – just as today the use of 'may' and 'might' to differentiate realized from hypothetical possibilities is distinctive of the older generation, and the use of undifferentiated 'may' of the younger (as is a worrying tendency to elide the personal 'who' and 'whom' into an undifferentiated neuter 'which').

Hope's method is useful in discriminating between collaborators, especially when each is represented by a large corpus of non-collaborative work, as is the case with Shakespeare, Middleton and Fletcher. He has been able to refine in detail on the conventional divisions of *Henry VIII* and *The Two Noble Kinsmen*; he finds it unlikely on linguistic evidence that *Double Falsehood* could be an eighteenth-century forgery; and he endorses the presence of Middleton in parts of

Timon of Athens. With the 'apocryphal' plays he is more tentative. Shakespeare is shown to be an impossible, or at least highly improbable, candidate for authorship of most of them, but Hope finds indications of possible collaboration in the writing of *The London Prodigal* and of the original text of *Sir Thomas More*. Of the plays he considers, only *King Edward III* falls consistently within the range of Shakespeare's usage employed for comparison.

The year 1999 saw an international wave of interest in *The Reign of King Edward III*. It was the subject of a long and informative programme on Japanese television in April; in the same month it was discussed on CBI Radio One in Canada in preparation for a radio reading of the play. It was given a public reading by members of the Royal Shakespeare Company at The Other Place in Stratford-upon-Avon in October, ten days before the first ever German production of *Die Regierung des Königs Edward III* opened at the municipal theatre of Cologne. The interest no doubt stemmed from the 1998 publication in the New Cambridge Shakespeare of Giorgio Melchiori's enthusiastic and illuminating edition of the play.

It seems to me that the time has come both to narrow and intensify the study of Shakespeare 'Apocrypha', and to widen our sense of the valid meanings of a Shakespeare 'canon'. Editions of the plays most plausibly regarded as having claims to be his, in whole or in part, are now increasingly available. The publication of such editions is a prerequisite for further scrutiny of the plays (not least in the theatre, where one recent candidate, *Edmond Ironside*, misleadingly promoted by Eric Sams as 'Shakespeare's lost play', nosedived in 1985 and has been little heard of since[80]). *The Two Noble Kinsmen* is now widely available; *Edward III* can be found in two good editions; the whole of *Sir Thomas More* has been twice edited by the indefatigable Professor Melchiori and his colleague Vittorio Gabrieli (in Italy in 1981 and in Britain in 1990).

Figure 9 *Edward III*, directed by Frank-Patrick Steckel, at the Bühnen der Stadt, Köln, 1999; Jochen Tovote as the King, Dagmar Sachse as the Countess

Of the plays most concerned, *Double Falsehood* alone is not yet readily available; but this, together with *Edward III* and *Sir Thomas More*, is projected for inclusion in the third series of the Arden Shakespeare.

~

In 1598 'William Shakespeare' was becoming a familiar, and so a commercially valuable, name in London; by 1609 it could appear without the 'William' on the title-page of *Shakespeare's Sonnets*. When William Shakespeare died, only half of the plays we know as his were in print. He may or may not have speculated about a collected edition of them. When that collection was published, posthumously, it was dedicated as a personal homage and memorial to a dear friend and colleague. Its title-page is dominated by the engraved portrait that remains the most familiar icon of the dramatist and that shows him simply as a man in contemporary dress, unframed and uncluttered by comment or decoration. Ben Jonson's verses on the facing page admonish us to 'looke / Not on his Picture, but his Booke'. The book remains his, and testifies to a memorable talent – a talent whose full development owed everything to the conditions of the man's life, not least his unparalleled good fortune in working for twenty or more years for the same acting company, in writing his plays for the talents of the best actors in England and in knowing that those plays would be performed.

At the beginning of the twenty-first century, I celebrate a moment when older certainties have yielded to a new openness (even, at times, a new humility) in the study and editing of Shakespeare. I celebrate a London in which there is once more a Globe playhouse on the south bank of the Thames, and a world in which we cannot travel far in any direction without encountering performances of Shakespeare's plays (and some 'Apocrypha'), in English or in one of the more than ninety-five other languages into which, David

Kastan assures us, they have been translated.[81] I also celebrate William Shakespeare and his book, reflecting that, if we wish to value his work, we should pay attention both to what it is still (just) permissible to call his 'genius'[82] and to the theatrical world that nurtured it.

NOTES

Place of publication is London unless otherwise stated.

CHAPTER 1 TEXT

1 *Much Ado about Nothing*, ed. G.R. Trenery (1924), xxii.

2 Quoted from four publicity pages bound in at the back of *Measure for Measure*, ed. H.C. Hart (1905), [4]. Advertisements bound into the back of several volumes give some sense of the passage of time. A '*new and cheaper issue*', initiated in 1905, lowered the price to 2*s.* 6*d.*, which remained the price of all 33 volumes listed in 1912. By 1918 it had risen to 3*s.*; and by 1924 this had doubled to 6*s.* (except for *A Midsummer Night's Dream* and *The Winter's Tale* at an unexplained 5*s.*). Readers requiring a complete set of Shakespeare could take the cheaper courses of choosing Methuen's 10-volume set at 6*d.* a volume in paper or 1*s.* in cloth, or 'The Little Quarto Shakespeare', edited by W.J. Craig, with introductions and notes, in 40 volumes ('*Pott 16mo.*', '*Leather, price 1s. net each volume. Mahogany Revolving Book Case. 10s. net.*').

3 'Some opinions of the press', in *Measure for Measure*, ed. Hart, [1].

4 A.J. West, 'Provisional new census of the Shakespeare First Folio', *The Library*, 6th series, 17 (1995), 60–73.

5 P.W.M. Blayney, *The First Folio of Shakespeare* (Washington, DC, 1991), 8.

6 Ibid., 6, 29, 32.

7 R. Dutton, *Ben Jonson: To the First Folio* (Cambridge, 1983), Introduction, 'The 1616 Folio and its place in Jonson's career', 1–22; *Ben Jonson, Authority, Criticism* (Basingstoke, New York, 1996), 61–9; D. Riggs, *Ben Jonson* (Cambridge, Mass., 1989), 220–39.

8 Blayney, *The First Folio*, 1.

9 British Library, MS. Harley 7368.

10 *Records of the Court of the Stationers' Company, 1576 to 1602, from Register B*, ed. W.W. Greg and E. Boswell (1930); *Records of the Court of the Stationers' Company, 1602 to 1640*, ed. W.A. Jackson (1930); D.F. McKenzie, 'A list of printers' apprentices, 1605–1640', *Studies in Bibliography*, 13 (1960), 109–41, and *Stationers' Company Apprentices 1641–1700* (Oxford, 1974).

11 E. Arber, *A Transcript of the Registers of the Company of Stationers of London, 1554–1640 A.D.*, 3 (1876), 170.

12 *Antony and Cleopatra*, 5.2.90.

13 W.W. Greg, *A Bibliography of English Printed Drama to the Restoration*, 4 vols (1939–59).

14 A.W. Pollard and G.R. Redgrave, *A Short-Title Catalogue of Books Printed in England, Scotland, & Ireland And of English Books Printed Abroad, 1475–1640* (London, 1926); 2nd edition, revised and enlarged, begun by W.A. Jackson and F.S. Ferguson, completed by K.F. Pantzer, 3 vols (1976–91).

15 C. Hinman, *The Printing and Proof-Reading of the First Folio of Shakespeare*, 2 vols (Oxford, 1963); P.W.M. Blayney, *The Texts of 'King Lear' and their Origins*, vol. 1: *Nicholas Okes and the First Quarto* (Cambridge, 1982).

16 *The Norton Facsimile: The First Folio of Shakespeare*, prepared by C. Hinman (1968); 2nd edition, with a new introduction by P.W.M. Blayney (1996).

17 Private comment to the author by J.W. Crow on publication of the Norton facsimile in 1968: inevitable human error saw to it that one page of the facsimile, p. 656, reproducing *Titus Andronicus*, fol. 2d^v, was reproduced from the uncorrected rather than the corrected state, the word 'hollow' at Through Line Number 1223 appearing with the two 'l's printing upside-down.

18 *Norton Facsimile* (1968), xxii–iv.

19 J. Moxon, *Mechanick Exercises on the Whole Art of Printing (1683–4)*, ed. H. Davis and H. Carter (Oxford, 1958), 233–9.

20 Hinman, *The Printing and Proof-Reading of the First Folio of Shakespeare*, vol. 2, 313–18.

21 S. Wells and G.Taylor, with J. Jowett and W. Montgomery, *William Shakespeare, A Textual Companion* (Oxford, 1987), 148–54.

22 Blayney, *The First Folio*, 17, 21–4.

23 C. Hinman, 'The prentice hand in the Shakespeare First Folio: Compositor E', *Studies in Bibliography*, 9 (1957), 3–20; F.T. Bowers, *Bibliography and Textual Criticism* (Oxford, 1964), 179–97, referring to D.F. McKenzie, 'A list of printers' apprentices', 125.

24 E.K. Chambers, 'The disintegration of Shakespeare', The British Academy Annual Shakespeare Lecture (1924), 22.

25 *Works*, ed. W.G. Clark and J. Glover, 9 vols (Cambridge, 1863–6), vols 2–9, ed. W.G. Clark and W.A. Wright.

26 A.W. Pollard, *Shakespeare Folios and Quartos: A Study in the Bibliography of Shakespeare's Plays 1594–1685* (1909), ch. 3, 'The good and the bad quartos', 64–80.

27 H.C. Bartlett and A.W. Pollard, *A Census of Shakespeare's Plays in Quarto, 1594–1709* (New Haven, Conn., 1916); rev. edn, ed. H.C. Bartlett (New Haven, Conn., 1939).

28 *Henslowe's Diary*, ed. W.W. Greg (1904); *Henslowe Papers*, ed. W.W. Greg (1907).

29 *Sir Thomas More*, ed. W.W. Greg (Oxford, 1911).

30 W.W. Greg, *The Editorial Problem in Shakespeare* (Oxford, 1942) and *The Shakespeare First Folio* (Oxford, 1955); R.B. McKerrow, *Prolegomena for the Oxford Shakespeare* (Oxford, 1939).

31 *The Works of Thomas Nashe*, ed. R.B. McKerrow, 5 vols (1904–10).

32 *The Works of Shakespeare,* ed. Sir A. Quiller-Couch and J.D. Wilson, with others (Cambridge, 1921–62).

33 F.T. Bowers, *On Editing Shakespeare and the Elizabethan Dramatists* (1955); *Bibliography and Textual Criticism* (Oxford, 1964); *On Editing Shakespeare* (Charlottesville, Va., 1966).

34 A. Walker, *Textual Problems of the First Folio* (Oxford, 1953).

35 S. Wells, J. Jowett and W. Montgomery, *William Shakespeare: A Textual Companion* (Oxford, 1987).

36 The Oxford Shakespeare uses the earlier titles *The First Part of the Contention* and *Richard Duke of York* for the plays printed in F as the second and third parts of *King Henry VI* and prefers the title *All Is True*, attested by contemporary references, to F's *The Life of King Henry VIII*; see H.R. Woudhuysen, '*King Henry VIII* and *All Is True*', *Notes & Queries*, 229 (1984), 217–18.

37 S. Wells and G. Taylor, *Modernizing Shakespeare's Spelling, with Three Studies in the Text of 'Henry V'* (Oxford, 1979); G. Taylor and J. Jowett, *Shakespeare Reshaped, 1606–1623* (Oxford, 1993).

38 *Riverside Shakespeare*, ed. G. Blakemore Evans (Cambridge, Mass., 1974; rev. 1997).

39 V. Salmon, 'The spelling and punctuation of Shakespeare's time', in *William Shakespeare, The Complete Works, Original-Spelling Edition* (Oxford, 1986), xlii–lvi.

40 W.W. Greg, 'The rationale of copy-text', *Studies in Bibliography*, 3 (1950–1), 19–36, repr. in *Collected Papers*, ed. J.C. Maxwell (Oxford, 1966), 374–91.

41 *The Most Excellent and Lamentable Tragedie of Romeo and Juliet*, A Critical Edition, ed. G.W. Williams (Durham, NC, 1964).

42 *Shakespeare Studies*, 24 (1996), 'Forum: editing early modern texts', 21–78, esp. S. Orgel, 'What is an editor?', 23–9, and P. Werstine, 'Editing after the end of editing', 47–54.

43 Margreta de Grazia, 'The essential Shakespeare', *Textual Practice*, 2 (1988), 71.

44 See e.g. B. Vickers, *Appropriating Shakespeare: Contemporary Critical Quarrels* (New Haven, Conn., and London, 1993), 406–16; I. Kamps, *Materialist Shakespeare: A History* (1995).

45 A.E. Housman, 'The application of thought to textual criticism' (1921), repr. in *Selected Prose*, ed. J. Carter (Cambridge, 1961), 131.

46 *Othello*, 1.3.145.

47 For studies of Compositor E, see Hinman, 'The prentice hand in the Shakespeare First Folio: Compositor E', 3–20; Bowers, *Bibliography and Textual Criticism*, 179–97, referring to McKenzie, 'A list of printers' apprentices', 125.

48 Blayney, *The Texts of 'King Lear' and their Origins*, vol. 1, ch. 8, 'Printers' copy'; J.K. Moore, *Primary Materials Relating to Copy and Print in English Books of the Sixteenth and Seventeenth Centuries* (Oxford, 1992).

49 Pollard, *Shakespeare Folios and Quartos*, 64–80.

50 A. Thompson and N. Taylor, '"O that this too too xxxxx text would melt": *Hamlet* and the indecisions of modern editors and publishers', *Text*, 10 (1999), 223.

51 *King Lear*, ed. G.I. Duthie (Cambridge, 1960); *Othello*, ed. J.D. Wilson and A. Walker (Cambridge, 1957); *Troilus and Cressida*, ed. A. Walker (Cambridge, 1957).

52 *Works*, ed. L. Theobald, 7 vols (1733), vol. 5, 103–219.

53 M.J. Warren, 'Quarto and Folio *King Lear* and the interpretation of Albany and Edgar', *Shakespeare, Pattern of Excelling Nature*, ed. D. Bevington and J.L. Halio (Newark, Del., 1978), 95–107.

54 See e.g. S. Urkowitz, *Shakespeare's Revision of 'King Lear'* (Princeton, NJ, 1980); G. Taylor and M. Warren (eds), *The Division of the Kingdoms* (Oxford, 1983).

55 *The Complete 'King Lear', 1608–1623*, ed. M. Warren (Berkeley, Los Angeles and London, 1989).

56 *William Shakespeare, The Complete Works* (Oxford, 1986): *The History of King Lear*, 1025–61; *The Tragedy of King Lear*, 1063–98.

57 J.J. McGann, *A Critique of Modern Textual Criticism* (Chicago, 1983; repr. Charlottesville, Va., 1992).

58 Ibid., 104–5.

59 *Hamlet*, ed. P. Edwards (Cambridge, 1985); ed. G. Taylor and S.W. Wells (Oxford, 1986), in *Complete Works*; ed. G.R. Hibbard (Oxford, 1987).

60 Videos of these films have been issued by Rank Home Video (Olivier: n.d.) and Columbia Tristar (Branagh: 1998).

61 This extract corresponds to 1.4.23–36.

62 4.4.32–66.

63 F.P. Wilson *Shakespeare and the New Bibliography*, rev. H. Gardner (Oxford, 1979), 62–4.

64 T.H. Howard-Hill, *Ralph Crane and Some Shakespeare First Folio Comedies* (Charlottesville, Va., 1972); E.A.J. Honigmann, *The Texts of 'Othello' and Shakespearian Revision* (1996).

65 This edition of *Hamlet* for the Arden Shakespeare, 3rd series, is projected for publication in 2002.

66 e.g. *The Tempest*, ed. S. Orgel (Oxford, 1987); *The Winter's Tale*, ed. S. Orgel (Oxford, 1996).

67 S. Johnson, 'Prologue spoken at the opening of the Theatre in Drury-Lane', ll. 51–4, *The Yale Edition of the Works of Samuel Johnson*, vol. 6: *Poems*, ed. E.L. McAdam, Jr, with G. Milne (New Haven, Conn., and London, 1964), 89.

68 *Othello*, 1.1.23–6.

69 *Shakespeare's Sonnets*, ed. S. Booth (New Haven, Conn., and London, 1977).

70 *Arden Shakespeare CD-ROM: Texts and Sources for Shakespeare Studies* (Walton-on-Thames, 1997).

71 *The Tempest*, 4.1.122–4, reproduced from the Norton Facsimile of the First Folio in Figure 2, p. 10.

72 *The Tempest*, ed. A. and V. Vaughan (Walton-on-Thames, 1999), 136–8.

73 J.A. Roberts, '"Wife" or "wise" – *The Tempest*, l. 1786', *Studies in Bibliography*, 31 (1978), 203–8.

74 *The Tempest*, ed. Vaughan, 137.

CHAPTER 2 STAGE

1 The audience at the Bear Garden Museum, where the lecture was given, included such eminent theatre scholars as C. Walter Hodges and Andrew Gurr.

2 Pentagram, the architects of the Globe, played host to a series of short colloquia and conferences at which controversial aspects of the rebuilding were discussed and decisions of principle taken in the years leading up to the rebuilding.

3 J.R. Mulryne and M. Shewring, *Shakespeare's Globe Rebuilt* (Cambridge, 1997), 15.

4 Thomas Platter's account is printed by E.K. Chambers, *The Elizabethan Stage*, 4 vols (Oxford, 1923), vol. 2, 364–5.

5 *All's Well that Ends Well*, 2.2.16–18.

6 F.P. Wilson, 'The Elizabethan theatre' (1955), repr. in H. Gardner (ed.), *Shakespearian and Other Studies* (Oxford, 1969), 198.

7 R. Proudfoot, 'Respecting the narrative', *Around the Globe*, 11 (Autumn 1999), 4–7.

8   R. Proudfoot, 'The 1998 Globe season', *Shakespeare Survey 52* (Cambridge, 1999), 215–28.

9   R. Speaight, *Shakespeare on the Stage: An Illustrated History of Shakespearian Performance* (1973), 239.

10   Ibid.

11   *Henslowe's Diary*, ed. R.A. Foakes and R.K. Rickert (Cambridge, 1961), 16–20, 21–2.

12   See E.K. Chambers, *William Shakespeare: A Study of Facts and Problems*, 2 vols (Oxford, 1933), vol. 2, 319–20, 327–8.

13   A. Gurr, *The Shakespearean Playing Companies* (Oxford, 1996; repr. 1999), 284.

14   S. McMillin and S.-B. MacLean, *The Queen's Men and their Plays* (Cambridge, 1998).

15   *Records of Early English Drama* (Toronto, Buffalo, London, 1979–).

16   J.A.B. Somerset, '"How chances it they travel?": provincial touring, playing places, and the King's Men', *Shakespeare Survey 47* (Cambridge, 1994), 45–60.

17   McMillin and MacLean, *The Queen's Men*, 82; see also J.H. Astington, *English Court Theatre, 1558–1642* (Cambridge, 2000).

18   R. Hosley, 'The playhouses', in J. Leeds Barroll, A. Leggatt, R. Hosley and A. Kernan, *The Revels History of Drama in English*, vol. 3: *1576–1603* (1975), 176, 181.

19   Chambers, *The Elizabethan Stage*, 4 vols (Oxford, 1923) vol. 2, 437.

20   Ibid., 466.

21   R.L. Knutson, *The Repertory of Shakespeare's Company, 1594–1613* (Fayetteville, Ark., 1991), ch. 4, 'The repertoire of the King's Men, 1603–1608'.

22   Twentieth-century scholarly editions of plays from the Globe repertoire include the following: *Ben Jonson*, ed. C.H. Herford, P. and E. Simpson, vol. 3: *Every Man in his Humour* (1927), vol. 4: *Sejanus* (1932) and vol. 5: *Volpone* (1937); [Thomas Middleton], *The Revenger's Tragedy*, ed. R.A. Foakes (1966); [Thomas Middleton], *A Yorkshire Tragedy*, ed. B. Gaines (1986); Thomas Dekker, *Dramatic Works*, ed. F.T. Bowers, vol. 1 (1953): *Satiromastix*; B. Barnes, *The Devil's Charter*, ed. R.B. McKerrow, in W. Bang, *Materialien zur Kunde des älteren Englischen Dramas* (1904); G. Wilkins, *The Miseries of Enforced Marriage*, ed. G.H. Blayney (Oxford, 1964); *A Larum for London*, ed. W.W. Greg (Oxford, 1913); *Thomas Lord Cromwell, The London Prodigal, The Merry Devil of Edmonton*, ed. C.F. Tucker Brooke, in *The Shakespeare Apocrypha* (Oxford, 1908); *The Fair Maid of Bristol*, ed. A.H. Quinn (Philadelphia, 1902).

23   The 'pulpit' in *Julius Caesar* 3.2 is interpreted as 'possibly ... the upper level (gallery) of the Globe' by D. Daniell in his Arden edition (1998), note on 3.2.11. It was effectively so staged at the new Globe in 1999.

24 Hosley, in *Revels History*, vol. 3, 191. I am indebted to Professor Andrew Gurr, in his words of thanks after my lecture at the Globe, for pointing out that experience at the reconstructed Globe demonstrates that trumpets, at least, could not have been played within the tiring-house, as their effect is totally deafening at such close quarters. It may be added that we have no detailed information about the structure or internal arrangements of an Elizabethan tiring-house and that this inconvenience might be avoided by experiment with different locations for the trumpeter.

25 Hosley, in ibid., 192.

26 Ibid., 193.

27 *A Larum*, E4^v–F1, lines 1310–36.

28 *The Devil's Charter*, sigs A2^v, F4, G1^v–2, M2^v.

29 Ibid., title-page, sig. A1.

30 See A.W. Pollard, *Shakespeare Folios and Quartos: A Study in the Bibliography of Shakespeare's Plays 1594–1685* (1909), ch. 3, 'The good and the bad quartos', 64–80.

31 *Hamlet* (1603), D4^v–E1.

32 L.E. Maguire, *Shakespearean Suspect Texts* (Cambridge, 1996).

33 Ibid., 324–5; for a reading of the 'bad' quartos as abridged acting texts, see R.E. Burkhart, 'Deliberate abridgements designed for performance by a reduced cast', *Shakespeare's Bad Quartos* (The Hague, 1975).

34 *Shakespeare's Merry Wives of Windsor 1602*, ed. W.W. Greg (Oxford, 1910), xl–xli.

35 G.I. Duthie, *Elizabethan Shorthand and the First Quarto of 'King Lear'* (Oxford, 1949); Maguire, *Shakespearean Suspect Texts*, ch. 4, 'Reporting speech, reconstructing texts', 95–112; but see also the reappraisal of the topic by A. Davidson in '"Some by stenography"? Stationers, shorthand, and the early Shakespearean quartos', *Papers of the Bibliographical Society of America*, 90 (1994), 417–49.

36 P.W.M. Blayney, 'The publication of playbooks', in J.D. Cox and D.S. Kastan (eds), *A New History of Early English Drama* (New York, 1997), 383–422.

37 *The Norton Facsimile* (1968), 7.

38 *Shakspere's Hamlet: The First Quarto, 1603* and *Shakspere's Hamlet: The Second Quarto, 1604*, facsimiles in photo-lithography by W. Griggs, with forewords by F.J. Furnivall [1880].

39 R. Speaight, *William Poel and the Elizabethan Revival* (1954), 48.

40 *Hamlet, The First Quarto* [1880], x.

41 Speaight, *William Poel*, 49–50.

42   Ibid., 48: Poel quotes from Q1 *Hamlet* (1603), C2^v and *Twelfth Night* 2.4.18–19.

43   Speaight, *William Poel*, 50.

44   Ibid., 51.

45   Ibid.

46   Dutton Cook, *Nights at the Play*, vol. 2 (1883), 314–16; repr. in Speaight, *William Poel*, 51.

47   Ibid.

48   See M. White, 'William Poel's Globe', *Theatre Notebook*, 53 (1999), 146–62.

49   G. Holderness and B. Loughrey, General Introduction, in *The Tragicall Historie of Hamlet Prince of Denmarke* (1992), 7.

50   T. Clayton (ed.), *The 'Hamlet' First Published: Q1 (1603)* (Newark, Del., 1992).

51   S. Urkowitz, 'Back to basics: thinking about the *Hamlet* First Quarto', in Clayton (ed.), *The 'Hamlet' First Published*, 257–91.

52   K.O. Irace, 'Origins and agents of *Q1 Hamlet*', in Clayton (ed.), *The 'Hamlet' First Published*, 90–122, and *Reforming the 'Bad' Quartos: Performance and Provenance of Six Shakespearean First Editions* (Newark, Del., 1994).

53   S. McMillin, 'Casting the *Hamlet* quartos: the limit of eleven', in Clayton (ed.), *The 'Hamlet' First Published*, 179–94.

54   Ibid., 190.

55   Prepared by J. Levenson and B. Gaines (Oxford, 2000).

56   Prepared by S.R. Miller (Oxford, 1998).

57   *The Taming of a Shrew: The 1594 Quarto*, ed. S.R. Miller, The New Cambridge Shakespeare, The Early Quartos (Cambridge, 1998).

58   B. Loughrey, 'Q1 in recent performance: an interview', in Clayton (ed.), *The 'Hamlet' First Published*, 125.

59   Clayton (ed.), *The 'Hamlet' First Published*, 291, n. 14.

60   S. Johnson, *Mr. Johnson's Preface to his Edition of Shakespear's Plays* (1765), xxvii.

61   I am indebted to Dr Martin Wiggins for reminding me that in 1608 the fourth quarto of *Richard II*, which is the earliest to print the deposition scene in 4.1, does specify the Globe as the place of performance on its title-page (as does the fifth quarto in 1615).

62   A3; *The Norton Facsimile* (1968), 7.

63   D.F. Rowan, 'A neglected Jones/Webb theatre project: Barber-Surgeons' Hall writ large', *New Theatre Magazine*, 9, 3 (Summer 1969), 6–15 (abstracted in *Shakespeare Survey 23* (1970), 125–30); 'A neglected Jones/Webb theatre project, part II: a theatrical missing link', in D. Galloway (ed.), *The Elizabethan Theatre II* (Toronto, 1970), 65.

64 J. Orrell, 'Inigo Jones at the Cockpit', *Shakespeare Survey 30* (1977), 157–68.

65 Gurr, *Shakespearean Playing Companies*, 294.

66 Chambers, *Elizabethan Stage*, vol. 2, 419–23; H.R. Woudhuysen, '*King Henry VIII* and *All Is True*', *Notes & Queries*, 229 (1984), 217–18.

67 Mulryne and Shewring, *Shakespeare's Globe Rebuilt*, 89, fig. 31 caption.

CHAPTER 3 CANON

1 W.E.Y. Elliott and R.J. Valenza, 'And then there were none: winnowing the Shakespeare claimants', *Computers and the Humanities*, 30 (1996), 191.

2 'Shall I die? Shall I fly ...?' first had the name of Shakespeare attached to a transcript of it in a manuscript collection of poems, now in the Bodleian Library, Oxford, dating from the 1630s. The attribution was first taken seriously by G. Taylor in parallel articles, including an edited text of the poem, in *The New York Times Book Review*, 15 December 1985, 11–14, and *The Times Literary Supplement*, 20 December 1985; it was included in the Oxford *Complete Works* (Oxford, 1986), 883. *A Funerall Elegye*, 'by W. S.' (1612), was first associated with Shakespeare by D.W. Foster in *Elegy by W. S.: A Study in Attribution* (Newark, Del., 1989) and was included in the second edition of *The Riverside Shakespeare* (Boston, New York, 1997), 1893–1904.

3 B. Vickers, *Appropriating Shakespeare* (New Haven, Conn., and London, 1992), 101–15, 489.

4 Cf. Geoffrey Hartman, 'English as something else', in S. Gubar and J. Kamholz (eds), *English Inside and Out* (New York and London, 1993), 38; H. Felperin, *The Uses of the Canon: Elizabethan Literature and Contemporary Theory* (Oxford, 1991); P. Kewes, *Authorship and Appropriation: Writing for the Stage in England, 1660–1710* (Oxford, 1998); J.A. Masten, 'Beaumont and/or Fletcher: collaboration and the interpretation of Renaissance drama', in M. Woodmansee and P. Jaszi (eds), *The Construction of Authorship: Textual Appropriation in Law and Literature* (Durham, NC, and London, 1994), 361–81.

5 *The Shakespeare Apocrypha*, ed. C.F. Tucker Brooke (Oxford, 1908).

6 H. Levin, in *The Riverside Shakespeare* (Boston, Mass., 1974), 1.

7 *The Tragedy of Master Arden of Faversham* (1592), ed. M.L. Wine (1973); *A Pleasant Comedy of Fair Em, the Miller's Daughter of Manchester, with the Love of William the Conqueror* [1593], ed. S. Henning (New York, 1980); *Sir Thomas More*, ed. V. Gabrieli and G. Melchiori (Manchester, 1990); *The Reign of King Edward III* (1596), ed. G. Melchiori (Cambridge, 1998); *The Comedy of Mucedorus, the King's Son of Valencia, and Amadine, the King's Daughter of Aragon* (1598, 1610), ed. A. Jupin (New York, 1987); *The Puritan, or the Widow of Watling Street* (1607), ed. D. Hamilton (forthcoming in the Oxford edition of

Thomas Middleton); *A Yorkshire Tragedy* (1608), ed. A.C. Cawley and B. Gaines (Manchester, 1986); *The First Part of the Life of Sir John Oldcastle* (1600), ed. P. Corbin and D. Sedge, in *The Oldcastle Controversy* (Manchester and New York, 1991); *The Merry Devil of Edmonton* (1608), ed. W.A. Abrams (Durham, NC, 1942), ed. N. Bennett (2000); *The Birth of Merlin, or The Child Hath Found His Father* (1662), ed. J. Udall (1991); *The Two Noble Kinsmen* (1634), ed. E.M. Waith (Oxford, 1989) and ed. L. Potter (Walton-on-Thames, 1997).

8 F.P. Wilson, *Shakespeare and the New Bibliography*, rev. H. Gardner (Oxford, 1979), 7–10.

9 A3; *The Norton Facsimile* (1968), 7.

10 A. Harbage, *Conceptions of Shakespeare* (1964), ch. 8, 'O blessed letters', 138–47, indulges in the pleasant fiction of a letter from Shakespeare recording the prophecy of Ben Jonson that Shakespeare's plays, like his own, will one day be printed in folio (144).

11 A2^v; *The Norton Facsimile* (1968), 6.

12 A8; *The Norton Facsimile* (1968), 17.

13 E.K. Chambers, *The Elizabethan Stage*, 4 vols (Oxford, 1923), vol. 2, 320–3, esp. 321.

14 *Sir Thomas More*, ed. Gabrieli and Melchiori (1990), 26–7.

15 P.W.M. Blayney, *The First Folio of Shakespeare* (Washington, DC, 1991), 17–24.

16 G.E. Bentley, *The Profession of Dramatist in Shakespeare's Time, 1590–1642* (Princeton, 1971), ch. 6, 'Dramatists' contractual obligations', 111–44.

17 First printed in the third edition, 1610: they show no internal evidence of Shakespeare's authorship.

18 See e.g. J. Hope, *The Authorship of Shakespeare's Plays* (Cambridge, 1994), 67–83; *King Henry VIII*, ed. G. McMullan (2000).

19 E. Malone, *A Dissertation on the Three Parts of King Henry VI. Tending to shew that those Plays were not written originally by Shakspeare* (1787).

20 E.K. Chambers, 'The disintegration of Shakespeare', The British Academy Annual Shakespeare Lecture (1924).

21 *William Shakespeare, The Complete Works* (Oxford, 1986), 893, 997, 1099.

22 e.g. G. Taylor, 'Shakespeare and others: the authorship of *Henry VI, Part 1*', *Medieval and Renaissance Drama in England*, 7 (1995), 145–205.

23 e.g. *Titus Andronicus*, ed. J.D. Wilson (Cambridge, 1948); McD.P. Jackson, *Studies in Attribution: Middleton and Shakespeare* (Salzburg, 1979).

24 A2, A3, A4; *The Norton Facsimile* (1968), 5, 7, 9.

25 R. Dutton, *Ben Jonson: To the First Folio* (Cambridge, 1983), Introduction, 'The 1616 Folio and its place in Jonson's career', 1–22; *Ben Jonson: Authority, Criticism*

(Basingstoke and New York, 1996), 61–9; D. Riggs, *Ben Jonson* (Cambridge, Mass., 1989), 220–39.

26 C. Hoy, 'The shares of Fletcher and his collaborators in the Beaumont and Fletcher canon', Parts 1–7, *Studies in Bibliography*, 8–9 (1956–7), 11–15 (1958–62).

27 John Fletcher and William Shakespeare, *The Two Noble Kinsmen*, ed. G.R. Proudfoot, Regents Renaissance Drama Series (Lincoln, Nebr., and London, 1970).

28 L.W. Hubbell, *A Note on the Shakespeare Apocrypha* (Kobe, 1977).

29 E.K. Chambers, *William Shakespeare: A Study of Facts and Problems* (Oxford, 1930), vol. 1, 537–9.

30 Rogers and Ley's catalogue, published with T. G., *The Careless Shepherdess* (1656), in W.W. Greg, *Bibliography of English Printed Drama to the Restoration*, 4 vols (1939–59), vol. 3, 1323.

31 Chambers, *William Shakespeare*, vol. 1, 539.

32 H. Moseley's entry dated 9 September 1653: 'The History of Cardenio, by M^r. Fletcher. and Shakespeare.', in Greg, *Bibliography*, vol. 1, 61.

33 Chambers, *William Shakespeare*, vol. 1, 539–42.

34 A1: 'Mr WILLIAM SHAKESPEAR'S Comedies, Histories, and Tragedies. Published according to the true Original Copies. *The third Impression.* And unto this Impression is added seven Playes, never before Printed in Folio. *viz. Pericles* Prince of *Tyre.* The *London Prodigall.* The History of *Thomas* L$^{d.}$ *Cromwell.* Sir *John Oldcastle* Lord *Cobham.* The *Puritan Widow.* A *York-shire* Tragedy. The Tragedy of *Locrine. LONDON,* Printed for *P. C.* 1664.'

35 *Supplement to the Edition of Shakspeare's Plays Published in 1778*, ed. E. Malone (1780), vol. 2, 189–90.

36 Ibid., 191.

37 *Double Falshood, or The Distrest Lovers*, ed. L. Theobald (1728), A5^v.

38 *Double Falshood, or The Distrest Lovers*, ed. L. Theobald, 2nd edition (1728), A5^v.

39 M. de Cervantes Saavedra, *Don Quixote*, tr. T. Shelton (1612), vol. 1, book 3, chs 9–10, 13; book 4, chs 1–3, 5, 9–10, 20; and perhaps book 2, chs 5, 24–5. G.H. Metz, *Sources of Four Plays Ascribed to Shakespeare* (Columbia, Mo., 1989), 294–370, prints all these sections in the text of the reprint by James Fitzmaurice-Kelly (1896), which is unfortunately based not on the 1612 edition of Shelton's version but on that of 1620, in which vol. 1 is a reprint and only vol. 2 was printed for the first time.

40 *Double Falshood, or The Distrest Lovers*, ed. Theobald (1728), A5, A5^v.

41 The first substantial defence of Theobald was by J. Freehafer, in '*Cardenio*, by Fletcher and Shakespeare', *Publications of the Modern Language Association of America*, 84 (1969), 501–13.

42 A.C. Sprague, *Beaumont and Fletcher on the Restoration Stage* (Cambridge, 1926), 129–37.

43 Freehafer, '*Cardenio*', 501–13.

44 S. Kukowski, 'The hand of Fletcher in *Double Falsehood*', *Shakespeare Survey 43* (1991), 81–9; A.L. Pujante, '*Double Falsehood* and the verbal parallels with Shelton's *Don Quixote*', *Shakespeare Survey 51* (1998), 95–105.

45 Freehafer, '*Cardenio*', 501–2.

46 B.S. Hammond, 'Theobald's *Double Falsehood*: an "agreeable cheat"?', *Notes & Queries*, 229 (1984), 2–3.

47 K. Muir, *Shakespeare as Collaborator* (1960), 157–8.

48 *Double Falsehood*, 1.2. 109–1 [B3^v].

49 R. Wilson, 'Unseasonable laughter: the context of *Cardenio*', in Jennifer Richards and James Knowles (eds), *Shakespeare's Late Plays* (Edinburgh, 1999), 193–209.

50 E. Capell, *Prolusions, or, select Pieces of antient Poetry* (1760), ix–x.

51 *King Edward III*, ed. G. Melchiori (Cambridge, 1998).

52 R. Speaight, *William Poel and the Elizabethan Revival* (1954), 73, 123.

53 *Edward III*, 2.1.451, and *Sonnets*, 94.14.

54 *The Book of Sir Thomas More*, ed. A. Dyce (1844), [v].

55 R. Simpson, 'Are there any extant MSS, in Shakespeare's handwriting?', *Notes & Queries*, 4th series, 8 (1871), 1–3.

56 *The Book of Sir Thomas More*, ed. W.W. Greg, Malone Society (Oxford, 1911).

57 Ibid., vii–x; see reprint (Oxford, 1961), Harold Jenkins, 'Supplement to the introduction', xxxiv–viii.

58 A.W. Pollard (ed.), *Shakespeare's Hand in 'The Book of Sir Thomas More'* (Cambridge, 1923).

59 J.M. Nosworthy, 'Shakespeare and *Sir Thomas More*', *Review of English Studies*, n.s., 6 (1955), 12–25.

60 J.D. Wilson, 'The spellings of the three pages, with parallels from the quartos', in Pollard (ed.), *Shakespeare's Hand*, 132–41.

61 T. Howard-Hill (ed.), *Shakespeare and 'Sir Thomas More': Essays on the Play and its Shakespearian Interest* (Cambridge, 1989), 8.

62 Ibid.

63 C.R. Forker, 'Webster or Shakespeare? Style, idiom, vocabulary and spelling in the additions to *Sir Thomas More*', in Howard-Hill (ed.), *Shakespeare and 'Sir Thomas More*', 151–70.

64 D. Bradley, *From Text to Performance in the Elizabethan Theatre* (Cambridge, 1992), ch. 4, 'The plotter at work', 75–94.

65 F. Meres, *Palladis Tamia: Wit's Treasury* (1598), fol. 283ᵛ, refers to him as '*Mundye our best plotter*'. In fairness, it should be added that when Ben Jonson, in *The Case is Altered*, lampooned Munday under the name of Antonio Balladino, it was as a prolific hack playwright that he ridiculed him. Balladino boasts, 'let me have a good ground, no matter for the pen, the plot shall carry it', to which his flatterer, Onion, replies, 'Indeed that's right, you are in print already for the best plotter' (*Ben Jonson*, ed. C.H. Herford, P. and E. Simpson, vol. 3 (Oxford, 1927), 108).

66 *John a Kent and John a Cumber*, ed. M.St.C. Byrne (Oxford, 1923).

67 G. Kane, *Piers Plowman: The Evidence for Authorship* (1965), 5–6.

68 G.R. Proudfoot, 'Shakespeare's most neglected play', in L.E. Maguire and T.L. Berger (eds), *Textual Formations and Reformations* (Newark, Del., and London, 1998), 149–57.

69 N. Bawcutt (ed.), *The Control and Censorship of Caroline Drama* (Oxford, 1996), 136: Astley was Herbert's immediate predecessor as censor of plays and later his assistant.

70 *A Critical, Old-Spelling Edition of 'The Birth of Merlin' (Q 1662)*, ed. J. Udall, Modern Humanities Research Association, Texts and Dissertations, vol. 31 (1991).

71 S. McMillin and S.-B. MacLean, *The Queen's Men and their Plays* (Cambridge, 1998), ch. 7, 'Marlowe and Shakespeare'.

72 G. Bullough, *Narrative and Dramatic Sources of Shakespeare*, 8 vols (1957–75).

73 e.g. A.Q. Morton, *Literary Detection: How to Prove Authorship and Fraud in Literature and Documents* (1978); F. Mosteller and D.L. Wallace, *Inference and Disputed Authorship: The Federalist* (Reading, Mass., 1964). Thomas Merriam (private communication) proposes that the more neutral 'logometry' might be a less confusing name for a technique that depends so heavily on counting words.

74 Hoy, 'The shares of Fletcher and his collaborators in the Beaumont and Fletcher canon'; D.J. Lake, *The Canon of Thomas Middleton's Plays* (Cambridge, 1975); McD.P. Jackson, *Studies in Attribution: Middleton and Shakespeare* (Salzburg, 1979).

75 e.g. W.E.Y. Elliott and R.J. Valenza, 'Glass slippers and seven-league boots: C–prompted doubts about ascribing *A Funeral Elegy* and *A Lover's Complaint* to Shakespeare', *Shakespeare Quarterly*, 48 (1997), 177–207.

76 Elliott and Valenza, 'And then there were none', 191. Minor revisions of their statistics, which affected none of their conclusions, were accepted by the authors after controversy with D.W. Foster: see D.W. Foster, 'The Shakespeare Authorship Clinic: how severe are the problems?', *Computers and the Humanities*, 32 (1999), 491–510; 'The professor doth protest too much, methinks: problems with the Foster "Response"', *Computers and the Humanities*, 32 (1999), 425–90.

77 Elliott and Valenza, 'And then there were none', 191.

78 R.A.J. Matthews and T.V.N. Merriam, 'Neural computation in stylometry I & II: an application to the works of Shakespeare and Fletcher', *Literary and Linguistic Computing*, 8 (1993), 203–9, and 9 (1994), 1–6; G. Ledger and T.V.N. Merriam, 'Shakespeare, Fletcher and *The Two Noble Kinsmen*', *Literary and Linguistic Computing*, 9 (1994), 135–48; D. Lowe and R.A.J. Matthews, Shakespeare vs. Fletcher: a stylometric analysis by radial basis functions', *Computers and the Humanities*, 29 (1995), 449–61; T.V.N. Merriam, '*Edward III*', *Literary and Linguistic Computing*, 15 (2000), 157–86

79 J. Hope, *The Authorship of Shakespeare's Plays* (Cambridge 1994).

80 *Ironside*, ed. E. Sams (1985): the play was performed at the Latchmere Theatre, Battersea, London, in 1985.

81 D.S. Kastan, *Shakespeare after Theory* (New York, London, 1999), 76.

82 J. Bate, *The Genius of Shakespeare* (Oxford, 1997).

INDEX

NOTE: Plays by or attributed to Shakespeare are entered individually under title. Page numbers in italic indicate information in a figure or caption; page numbers followed by *n* indicate information in a note.

114   *Shakespeare: Text, Stage and Canon*